So

GOING
TO BE
A PARENT

William Sears, M.D.
&
Martha Sears, R.N.

THOMAS NELSON PUBLISHERS
Nashville

Published in association with the literary agency of Alive Communications, 1465 Kelly Johnson Blvd., Suite #320, Colorado Springs, CO 80920.

Published in Nashville, Tennessee, by Thomas Nelson, Inc., Publishers.

Unless otherwise noted, Scripture quotations are from THE NEW KING JAMES VERSION. Copyright © 1979, 1980, 1982, 1990, Thomas Nelson, Inc., Publishers.

Scripture quotations noted NIV are from the HOLY BIBLE: NEW INTERNATIONAL VERSION®. Copyright © 1973, 1978, 1984 by International Bible Society. Used by permission of Zondervan Publishing House. All rights reserved.

Scripture quotations noted KJV are from the KING JAMES VERSION of the Bible.

Library of Congress Cataloging-in-Publication Data

Sears, William, M.D.
    [Christian parenting and child care]
    So you're going to be a parent / William Sears and Martha Sears.
       p. cm.—(The Sears parenting library)
    "Janet Thoma books."
    Originally published: Christian parenting and child care. Nashville : T. Nelson Publishers, c1991.
    Includes bibliographical references (p. 179) and index.
    ISBN 0-7852-7206-2 (pbk.)
    1. Family—Religious life. 2. Parenting—Religious aspects—Christianity. 3. Married people—Religious life. I. Sears, Martha. II. Title. III. Series: Sears, William, M.D. Sears parenting library.
BV4526.2.S43 1998
248.8′45—dc21   97–51881
                                        CIP

Printed in the United States of America
1 2 3 4 5 6 7 — 03 02 01 00 99 98

Contents

Preface

My dear Christian parents, this book arose out of my own deep love and concern for children as one of God's greatest gifts to us. A child is a gift for us to love, to nurture, and ultimately to return to Him a finished person.

Because they are such a precious gift, I feel that our Creator has given us a divine design for the care and feeding of His children. Over the past decade and a half, I have been increasingly concerned that this design is not being followed. As a result, parents are having difficulty training their children, who are departing from the way they should go. In The Sears Parenting Library I want to convey what I believe is God's design for parenting, and I will offer practical suggestions on how to follow that design.

During my past twenty years in pediatric practice I have carefully observed what parenting styles work for most parents most of the time. Besides learning from my patients, I have been blessed with a wonderful wife, Martha, who is a professional mother. If, after reading this book, you are more able to achieve the three goals of parenting, which are to know your child, to help your child feel right, and to lead your child to Christ, then I will have served my Lord in writing this book.

William P. Sears, M.D.
San Clemente, California

Introduction

The main purpose of *So You're Going to Be a Parent* is to help parents achieve what I believe are the three primary goals of Christian parenting:

1. To know your child
2. To help your child feel right
3. To lead your child to Christ

Each child comes wired with a unique set of characteristics called *temperament*. No two children come wired the same. Each child also has a certain level of needs that, if met, will enable him to reach his fullest potential. Some children have higher needs than others.

Each parent is endowed with a natural ability to nurture. Some children require more nurturing than others, and some parents have a higher level of giving than others. Implied in the concept of a loving Creator is that God would not give to parents a child they could not handle. God's matching program is perfect; His law of supply and demand will work if people practice a style of parenting that allows the divine design for the parent-child relationship to develop.

The term *parenting style* means "a way of caring for your child." Restrained parenting is one parenting style that is earmarked by phrases like, "Let your baby cry it out," "What, you're still nursing?" "Don't let him sleep with you," "Get him on a schedule," "You're making him too dependent," and "You're going to spoil her." These common admonitions from trusted advisers to vulnerable new parents keep them from fully enjoying their child.

The style of parenting I believe God designed for the care and feeding of His children is what I call "attachment parenting," which encourages new parents to respond to their child's cues without restraint. The fundamentals of attachment parenting include the eight baby Bs:

1. *Bonding.* Pray for your preborn baby during pregnancy. Also, unless a medical complication prevents it, keep your newborn in touch with you continuously, or at least as many hours a day as possible during the early weeks. Familiarity builds your confidence because it allows you to get to know your baby intimately.

2. *Breastfeeding.* This is an exercise in babyreading, helping you learn to read your baby's cues. Breastfeeding also stimulates an outpouring of the hormones prolactin and oxytocin. These mothering hormones act like biochemical helpers, which may also be the biological basis of God's design for the term *mother's intuition.*

3. *Babywearing.* Closeness promotes familiarity. Wear your baby in a babysling as many hours a day as you and your baby enjoy. Because baby is so close to you in your arms and in contact with you, you get to know your baby better. And your baby is calmer and easier to care for.

4. *Bedsharing.* Truly, there is no one right place for baby to sleep. Wherever all family members get the best sleep is the right arrangement for them, and that arrangement may vary at different stages of baby's development. Allowing baby to sleep next to you in your bed, especially in the early months, is valuable for busy parents who do not have much daytime contact with their baby. Bedsharing allows you to reconnect with your baby at night to make up for being out of touch during the day.

5. *Believe in baby's cries.* A baby's cry is a baby's language. It is designed for the survival of the baby and the development of the mother. If you listen to your baby's cries and needs when your infant is young, your child is likely to listen to your instructions later on.

6. *Building a support network.* Use the biblical model of veteran parents teaching novices. The support people around you can be a help in building your intuition or they can be a hindrance.

7. *Boundary building.* Practicing attachment parenting according to God's design implies knowing when to say yes and no to your infant and child. This is why throughout this series of books we emphasize discipline as a major part of Christian parenting.

8. *Balance.* Attachment parenting may sound like one big give-a-thon, in the long run it actually makes parenting a lot easier. The more you give to your child, the more your child gives back to you. Yet, focusing exclusively on your baby's needs and ignoring your own is not wise parenting. Periodically take inventory of your overall style of parenting. Ask yourself "Is it working for me?" and "Am I doing what I need to do for my own well-being?"

Attachment parenting early on makes later parenting easier, not only in infancy but in childhood and in your child's teenage years. The ability to read and respond to your baby carries over to the ability to get inside your child's mind and see things from her perspective. When you truly know your child, parenting is easier at all ages.

I arrived at these principles of attachment parenting not only from parenting eight children with my wife, Martha, but also from observing my patients for twenty years. I also have been encouraged by organizations, such as the La Leche League, that advocate similar parenting principles.

Practicing these principles can help you have a realistic expectation of childhood behavior. You will be more observant of your infant's cues and will be able to respond intuitively. As you become more confident in your ability to meet your baby's needs you will enjoy parenting more and more.

Because of the great variability in family situations, some parents may not be able to practice all of these disciplines all of the time. I just want to make the point that the more parents practice these styles, the greater is their opportunity of truly enjoying their child and of claiming the promise, "Train up a child in the way he should go, / And when he is old he will not depart from it" (Prov. 22:6).

What attachment parenting does for you may be summed up in one word—*harmony*. You and your baby will be more in sync with each other; you will become sensitive to your baby.

Mothers also undergo a chemical change when they have this harmony. Because they are breastfeeding and interacting with their babies, they receive more of the hormone prolactin. I call prolactin "the mothering hormone" because it gives mothers the added boost they need during those trying times.

Attachment parenting also gives your child a model to follow when he or she becomes a parent. Remember, you are parenting someone else's future husband, wife, father, or mother. How your child is parented may influence how he or she parents. The lack of a definite model is what causes confusion in many young parents today.

The principles of attachment parenting are especially rewarding for the parents of "fussy" or "demanding" children whom I like to call "high-need babies." We will be discussing the traits of high-need children and how to parent these special blessings.

There is a parallel between a child's relationship with his parents and his relationship with God. The parental relationship a child has in his early formative years has a direct bearing on his eventual relationship with God. If a child has learned trust, discipline, and love from his parents, he will be prepared to transfer these concepts to God. As you study the tenets of attachment parenting, you will see how to apply them to the spiritual training of your child.

In the following chapters, and in the other books in this series, the disciplines of attachment parenting are covered in great detail. For parents who wish to get the most out of this book, read the entire book through once, and you will see how all these attachment tips fit together. By the end of the book I hope parents will perceive these biblical concepts to be a Christian parenting style that is in accordance with God's design.

Part 1

Pregnancy

CHAPTER 1

MAKING IMPORTANT CHOICES

Upon learning that they are expecting a baby, couples must make several significant decisions in a relatively short period of time: choosing an obstetrician, pediatrician, place for and style of labor and delivery, and what type, if any, childbirth preparation classes to take. Because each family's needs and philosophies differ, there is no one right course to follow or decision to make, although I do believe some practices are more in accord with God's loving design for the family than others. Take some time to sort out your own beliefs and preferences, pray for wisdom, and then trust your judgment as you make these first important steps toward becoming parents.

Once your home pregnancy test delivers a positive result, you will need to choose an obstetrician. In perhaps no other medical specialty is the art of patient-doctor communication so important. Because of the intensely personal, vitally important, and extended nature of the pregnancy, labor, and delivery, it is essential that both partners are comfortable with the chosen physician or group practice. The following suggestions will guide you in selecting your obstetrician.

Choosing Your Obstetrician

If possible, select two or three doctors to interview based on insurance parameters, personal recommendations, or the doctor's credentials.

As with all of your major decisions throughout your parenting career, pray for wisdom that God may guide you in choosing the right doctor for you. In my opinion, an obstetrician should be 100 percent pro life—many women find it impossible to be attended at birth by a doctor who also terminates life.

When making your first appointment, let the obstetrician know you are making the appointment solely to discuss the doctor's philosophy of childbirth and his or her attitudes toward your needs. It is quite advisable and customary to interview doctors before choosing the right one for your family. Both parents-to-be should attend this first appointment.

When you first meet your prospective obstetrician, take a written list of questions specific to your needs. Some sample questions you may wish to ask include: We have the following concerns about our pregnancy and birth (name your specific concerns); what help can you offer us? Remember, the more frank and open you are with your obstetrician, the more sensitive he or she can be to your individual needs. What childbirth education classes do you recommend? Which hospital do you advise, and what are the alternative birthing concepts within that hospital? What are your policies concerning father involvement, mother-baby separation at birth, and rooming-in (or any other practices important to you)? Will you pray with us in time of need?

Because of the increasing numbers of prepared and discerning parents, most obstetricians are becoming more flexible about offering alternative methods of birthing to meet the parents' requests. As you ask your obstetrician to be sensitive to your needs, please be sensitive to your doctor. The physician you are speaking with is a highly trained medical professional who has a sincere interest in the medical safety of your childbirth. For this reason you will probably receive an answer like this, "I respect your desires completely, but I must, for the best medical interest of yourself and your baby, reserve the right to intervene medically should the need arise. You will have to trust my judgment." A Christian obstetrician may add, "We must pray that God will give us both the wisdom to trust each other's judgment." Your doctor is asking of you the same respect and flexibility that you are asking of him or her.

Choosing Your Pediatrician

When selecting your pediatrician, follow basically the same guidelines for choosing your obstetrician; consider the doctor's competence, communication abilities, and his or her walk with God. It is just as important to have a face-to-face interview with the pediatrician during pregnancy as it is to interview the obstetrician. Otherwise, your first meeting with the pediatrician will take place in the hospital shortly after delivery when he or she makes the initial examination of your newborn. This initial patient-doctor communication is often compromised by the confusion or hubbub of a busy hospital ward, an extremely tired mother, or a hurried doctor. For these reasons it is strongly advisable for you to interview your prospective pediatrician during the latter months of your pregnancy. This prenatal visit will give the pediatrician an idea of what you really want and also will increase his or her respect for you as prospective parents.

Bring a written list of your most pressing questions and concerns. Attempt to keep the interview brief since most pediatricians do not charge for this prenatal visit. Respect the doctor's time.

Ask your prospective pediatrician his or her philosophy about the aspects of child rearing that are most important to you. Ask your pediatrician what his or her schedule for routine examinations is and how he or she will be involved in the care of your baby in the hospital. How do you reach the doctor in case of emergency?

Avoid negative openers. Nothing is more nonproductive than opening the interview with a list of "I don't wants"; for example, "I don't want my baby to have any bottles in the hospital." It is more productive to ask, "What is your policy about giving bottles to breastfeeding babies in the hospital?" Remember, your purpose for the interview is to determine if you and your prospective pediatrician are on the same wavelength. Negative openers close your mind to the possibility that you may, in fact, learn something by your doctor's response, something you may not have considered before your interview although you were certain your mind was completely made up. Persistently negative openers may set up a barrier for trusting future communication.

To help you get the most out of your prenatal visit with your pediatrician, look at this visit through the doctor's eyes. All during the interview he or she is filing away bits of information from which he can draw his conclusions about his future level of service to you. A sample thought process of an intuitive pediatrician would be: *These parents are certainly off to the right start. Parenting seems to be a top priority in their lives at this moment. They have taken time to interview me, and I can tell from their questions that choosing a pediatrician for their baby is also a high priority. These parents care, which makes me want to care. Therefore, I will make a special effort to be a good pediatrician for them.*

A caring pediatrician and intuitive parents are a winning combination that brings to your child a level of pediatric care that most parents and children want and deserve. Some parents feel confident enough in their parenting that they want a lesser level of involvement of the pediatrician in their family; he is on standby should a medical problem arise. Other parents, especially first-time parents, often want a highly involved pediatrician, a sort of Uncle Harry who becomes a trusted extra member of the family.

One of my most memorable new-patient visits was from a couple who said to me, "We'll pray for you; we always pray for our doctors." That simple statement said it all. From then on I knew what level my relationship was to be with that family.

Choosing Where to Deliver Your Baby

One of the most exciting, long-overdue changes in obstetrics is the many childbirth choices available for today's couples. These various options are termed *alternative birthing concepts* or the ABCs of modern obstetrical medicine. Where and how you deliver your baby are probably two of the most important decisions you will make during your pregnancy. These decisions should be made with much prayer and consultation.

Many variables go into making the right decisions: Is this your first baby? Are you anticipating any obstetrical complications? What can you afford? How far do you live from your hospital or birth attendant? How important to you are the setting and the environment of your childbirth experience? The following options are available for you to consider.

1. *A traditional method of delivery.* I only mention this option to discourage it. Fortunately, gone are the days (or at least they should be) when birth was marketed as a disease and a woman went to the hospital to be relieved by means of a medical and/or surgical procedure. Natural childbirth classes were not encouraged. A father was made to feel unclean and inept and was banished into the waiting room while the mother labored and delivered alone. As in any routine surgery, the mother's perineum was shaved. (Fortunately studies have shown that this humiliating practice has no effect on lessening infection.) The lonely, laboring mother was required to remain on her back. (Laboring while lying on one's back is not only the position of maximal pain, but it is often the least beneficial position for the fetus because it lessens the blood flow to the uterus.) The mother was then medicated on an operating table and strapped into stirrups. After the birth, mother and baby were taken to separate rooms to "recover" from this operation of birth. A newborn baby was often kept in a bassinet, cared for by experts in the nursery, and brought to this mother only at convenient intervals. The father, meanwhile, viewed his baby through the glass windows of the nursery. The baby was fed a

scientifically tested formula that was supposed to be as good as and certainly more convenient than what the Creator had designed. Fortunately, nearly all couples today have the wisdom to demand more from the birth event than what these antiquated practices provide.

2. *Birthing or LDR rooms.* Most hospitals now offer a childbirth option called "labor, delivery, recovery" or "birthing room." It is located within the usual obstetrical ward of a hospital and is sometimes referred to as an ABC (alternative birth center). At first glance this room (or suite of rooms) looks like a normal bedroom and is designed to convey a homelike environment. Furnishings may include colorful curtains and bedspreads, plants, rocking chair, stereo, kitchenette, Jacuzzi, and similar conveniences. The bed does not look like a delivery table but resembles most hospital beds (or even a homey queen-size brass bed) and is adjustable for the laboring mother. Some rooms have birthing chairs. All the medical and surgical equipment that may be needed is unobtrusively but efficiently near at hand.

The laboring couple are admitted to the birthing room. They labor together in this room, deliver in this room, and spend their postpartum course in this room. They are not transported from room to room as they would be in "traditional" births. A very important feature of the birthing room is that the baby can stay with the mother from birth to discharge from the hospital and is taken into the nursery only if the mother wishes or medical complications occur. The birthing room represents more than just a physical facility. It represents an attitude that birth is a normal process in life until proven otherwise.

An important factor for an expectant couple to

consider in choosing a hospital is the level of newborn intensive care available should medical complications arise during or after birth. If a complication occurs around the time of birth, it is usually with the baby. Therefore, parents should base their choice of a hospital on the level of newborn care facilities as well as the facilities available for mother care.

3. *Birthing centers.* Freestanding birthing centers are located and run separately from any hospital but are usually within minutes of a medical facility where the laboring mother can be transported if complications arise. Birth centers are staffed by certified nurse midwives (or by lay midwives in some states) and have medical supervision. Some are even owned and operated by physicians who rely on midwives to provide some or most of the prenatal and birth services. In this type of birth environment couples can find the homelike setting so important to them without the restrictions still encountered in hospital birthing rooms. A well-trained and experienced midwife is the ideal birthing attendant because her mind-set is one that is dedicated to the concept that birth is a normal, healthy process for *at least* 90 percent of all women. She is also able to discern which women will need the services of an obstetrician and she is wise enough to screen her clientele carefully. Hospitals are beginning to recognize the value of midwives. This is good because I see that this is where the future of health care for expectant families lies. Many midwives are dedicated Christian women who see their profession as a ministry as God revealed in Scripture (Ex. 1:15–21).

4. *Home births.* The home-birth movement arose because the traditional system of maternal care failed to recognize an honest consumer need. Increasing num-

bers of couples have reacted to the childbirth-is-a-disease-needing-treatment-by-an-operation attitude by taking the birth event back to where it was in biblical days, the home.

Because of the possibility of obstetrical complications, both the American Academy of Obstetrics and Gynecology and the American Academy of Pediatrics advise against giving birth in the home. The person who has the highest risk, the baby, has no voice in this decision. I am in deep sympathy with couples who wish to give birth at home. I can speak with some insight into this dilemma, since four of our eight births were at home. It is a beautiful human experience for parents and baby. As with all the options of child-birthing environments, prayer and consultation are needed before choosing to have a home birth. I do acknowledge that there are couples whom God will lead toward properly attended home births. Perhaps the answer to this dilemma is a homelike birthing environment in the hospital or birthing center.

In summary, use prayerful discernment in deciding where to birth your baby. The option of childbirthing environments that I would encourage most expectant couples to choose would be a hospital that has both a genuine alternative birthing center for low-risk obstetrical patients and expert newborn care facilities for unanticipated medical complications. The choice between "natural" or "technological" childbirth should not be an either-or decision. I thank God for the technological advances that have saved the lives of many mothers and babies, but I feel that modern maternal care should be a blend of parental intuition and medical science. The parents and the baby should not be deprived of either one.

Natural Childbirth Classes

I highly recommend that as a first-time pregnant couple you enroll in a natural childbirth class around the sixth month of pregnancy. If possible, find a Christian childbirth class that teaches biblical principles to alleviate the fear of childbirth. Most hospital-based childbirth classes teach couples what the hospital and the doctors consider important. A better choice would be a reliable private teacher or a consumer-based organization that will help you prepare for the birth you want. The following list names the more popular organizations that teach childbirth classes. They differ mainly in the techniques of relaxation and coping with the stress of childbirth. Christian childbirth classes often incorporate the best techniques from these organizations.

1. Apple Tree Family Ministries—a Christian organization
2. The American Society for Psychoprophylaxis in Obstetrics (ASPO)—also known as the Lamaze method
3. The American Academy of Husband-Coached Childbirth—the Bradley method
4. International Childbirth Education Association (ICEA)
5. Alternative Childbirth Educators (ACE)

■ Natural Childbirth—What It Means, and Is It for You?

With so many birth options, the term *natural birth* means different things to different women. A mother in our practice once told us that for her, natural childbirth was going to the hospital without her makeup on. Others consider the term *natural childbirth* to mean a totally unmedicated and intervention-free birth. Yet, for some mothers this type of birth may be undesirable or medically impossible.

It's not what you call your birth that counts, but how you've prepared for it. The term *responsible childbirth* is a more realistic term. Responsible childbirth means that you trust that God designed your body to work. It means that you have studied your options, formulated a philosophy and plan of birth, put together a carefully chosen birth team, and armed yourself with the necessary information and techniques to birth your baby. When you enter your delivery with this powerful package, you can call your birth anything you want and have the comfort of knowing that you have had a responsible childbirth. ■

Christian Childbirth Classes

If you are properly and prayerfully prepared, your childbirth most often will be a good, natural experience. For Christian couples there is an added dimension of childbirth preparation with which they can equip themselves. God's promises for them in pregnancy and in childbirth are a tremendous source of strength and blessing, but a source that is often untapped. These scriptural promises will be explored in the following section.

Birth, marriage, and death are important events in

a person's life. No Christian would dream of approaching them without the support of prayer, Scripture, and fellowship. Christian childbirth classes combine the benefits of physical and emotional training with thorough spiritual preparation.

Overcoming Fear

Overcoming fear is one of the oldest and most effective helps in childbirth preparation. Dr. Grantly Dick-Read did the pioneer research on the effects of fear on women in childbirth. His research was not easily accepted by his professional colleagues because, at that time, the scientific answer to fear was anesthesia. In the 1940s Dr. Dick-Read published *Childbirth Without Fear* (now in its fifth edition), and as a result, *natural childbirth* became a household term. He knew instinctively that childbirth was not intended by God to be a time of severe suffering, and he recognized the role that fear played in making it so. This truth is borne out beautifully in God's Word. Scriptures refer to childbirth as a joyful time (Gen. 21:6–7; Luke 1:58; and John 16:21).

Helen Wessel, in her book *Natural Childbirth and the Christian Family,* researched the original Hebrew meaning of certain terms relating to childbirth. She showed how modern translators have done childbearing women a disservice. For example, Genesis 3:16 reads, "To the woman he said, 'I will greatly increase your pains in childbearing; with pain you will give birth to children'" (NIV). The word *pains* in the first half of the verse is translated from the Hebrew root word *itstsabon,* meaning "sorrow" or "toil"; it is actually referring to the mental state rather than to a strictly physical state. God was telling Eve that as a consequence of her disobedience she would have to work hard and struggle mentally and physically giving birth to children that He could have freely and easily given her had she not broken communion with Him by sinning. Today, women must also live with the toil of labor and with a mental state of concern that all will go well with the new little lives they are bringing forth.

■ Resource for Expectant Parents

A valuable resource for the pregnant couple is *The Pregnancy Book: A Month-by-Month Guide* by William and Martha Sears, with obstetrician Dr. Linda Hewey Holt.

In this monthly guide, expectant parents will be given the tools to increase their chances of having a safe and satisfying birth. This research is based upon our combined experience of Martha as a childbirth educator and mother of eight, Dr. Holt as an obstetrician, and Dr. Bill as a pediatrician. We have combined experiences of attending thousands of births and have learned what works for most laboring mothers most of the time. This book is especially a valuable resource for helping mothers work out a personal pain-management program, using the latest advances in both natural and medical pain relief. ■

To show how unfair some modern biblical translations are in treating this area of childbirth pain, consider Genesis 3:17 where God said to Adam, "Cursed is the ground because of you; through painful toil you will eat of it all the days of your life" (NIV). The word *toil* is translated from the same Hebrew word *itstsabon*. Cultural programming has caused the word to be translated *pain* concerning Eve but *toil* concerning Adam. Basically, God was telling Adam and Eve that having sinned, they both would have to work hard to bring forth the fruit they desired. The so-called curse of Eve in which women are supposed to be penalized by pain and suffering during childbirth actually has no scriptural basis.

To illustrate how some modern translators have perpetuated this myth, notice the difference in translations of Genesis 3:16 between the 1978 New International Version and the original King James Version. The KJV reads, "I will greatly multiply thy *sorrow* and thy conception; in *sorrow* thou shalt bring forth children" (italics added). The NIV reads, "I will greatly increase your *pains* in childbearing; with *pain* you will give birth to children" (italics added).

As you can see, there is nothing about physical pain and suffering in the King James translation. The term *sorrow* probably refers to the whole of motherhood, not birth. For example, think of the sorrow Eve must have felt when Cain killed Abel. Many Christian childbirth educators do not accept that a woman must suffer pain in childbirth; they teach expectant women not to expect severe pain and suffering during their birthing experiences.

We must be aware that hard work in labor is not "suffering" in labor any more than hard work in farming the land is suffering. Many childbirth educators feel that a mother benefits from being able to experience the full sensation of her body in labor. They feel that seeking to abolish all feeling denies the sensuality of birth. No one wants a mother to suffer during childbirth, but a mother may greatly regret a nonexperience. Some studies have suggested that the reality of seeing and feeling the entire birth experience has significant benefits for successful bonding in the newborn period and the mother's postpartum adjustments. However, a negative birth experience in which fear and pain predominate may also negatively affect a mother in postpartum adjustment.

Birth is hard work, as is running a hard race. The exertion is intense. At times during the race muscle pain is felt, similar to the "hurdler" pain that is felt during a highly competitive track meet. This is a productive, positive type of pain that drives the runner toward the finish line. It is far different from the pain of a traumatic sports injury that is negative and nonproductive.

Labor pain becomes suffering in one of two ways: either there is a high element of fear present, or there is a physical problem causing severe pain. Modern obstetrics is able to deal most effectively, and in a lifesaving way, with situations involving physical disease, malfunctions, or malpresentations. For example, a baby's head may not fit the space in which it has to maneuver for descent into the birth canal, no matter how hard and painfully the muscles work. In these situations a cesarean birth or some other form of intervention becomes *truly* necessary and we can thank our heavenly Father for the advances in technology that allow these mothers and babies to be helped. In fact, some form of medical or surgical intervention is necessary in about 5 percent of all births. It is to the other 95 percent of births that fear can become the enemy and produce a much larger percentage of problems. "Failure to progress" is the largest category of reasons for cesarean section.

Cesarean birth has become "epidemic" and now accounts for 25 percent of all births. Much attention is being given to reducing this percentage by professional committees and by lay organizations such as Cesarean Prevention Movement, Inc., P.O. Box 152, Syracuse, NY 13210.

Vaginal birth after cesarean (VBAC) is now an important option for women who have had a cesarean birth previously. The adage "once a cesarean always a cesarean" is no longer accepted by even the most conservative obstetricians. At least 70 percent of all previous cesarean births can be successful VBACs.

The natural birth process that God designed is one of the most awe-inspiring miracles witnessed. Only God could have figured out so intricately the way in which hormones, muscles, bony structures, and emotions interrelate in labor and birth. Even though God's design is so perfect, Satan can still rob women of the wonder and beauty of birth through deceitful fear. Fear and the resulting tension can lead to serious problems for mothers because they prevent labor from progressing, and for babies because they result in fetal distress. The use of drugs as the answer to the fear-tension-pain cycle is inadequate and unsafe. Instead, natural childbirth classes with a Christian emphasis are valuable as couples equip themselves to experience birth. Couples learn all they can about pregnancy, labor, and birth so that the fear of the unknown no longer can defeat them.

Fear works against the woman in the birth process. The birth muscles—the uterus and the birth passage—are designed to press forward and open the "baby door" gradually and smoothly so that there need be no suffering, only some really intense emotional and physical sensations. The idea is to coordinate the opening of the birth passage with the muscular contractions of the uterus so that the intense force does not become unbearably painful. If fear enters the process, tension results, and the muscles of the birth passage become rigid, causing terrible pain because the baby is pushed down against those hard, unyielding muscles.

Breaking the fear-tension-pain cycle at any one of several points greatly increases the ability to enjoy childbirth. By overcoming fear (especially the fear of the unknown), by learning why the physical sensations occur, by reducing the tension in muscle and mind produced by that fear, by using relaxation techniques, and by learning how to work *with* rather than against their bodies in labor, most women do not have to suffer or be drugged to give birth.

This is not to say that the birth process is painless, but natural childbirth classes teach you to interpret birth sensations for what they really are—part of the normal physiological process for which the female body was designed. Severe pain in childbirth is not normal but is a sign of an underlying problem, as severe pain is a sign that any normal body process is not operating properly. If that problem can be corrected (or avoided), intolerable pain can be reduced to the level of an acceptable sensation that you can tell feels right and is nothing to fear. If that problem cannot be corrected, then medical and surgical intervention is to be used appropriately and without condemnation.

What are some of the sources of fear? Where does this destructive emotion come from that takes over our minds and causes tension in our bodies? There are as many answers to these questions as there are women giving birth.

Fear of the unknown, based on horror stories

passed down from generations that did experience birth as a dreadful and sometimes fatal event, is one kind of fear. Perhaps these fears are further validated by a woman's own past unprepared labor experiences. Fear also can be based on an ambivalent attitude about the pregnancy—unwanted pregnancy, economic insecurity, husband-wife problems, unsupportive or interfering relatives. A woman also can have fears that her baby will not be normal or that she will not be a good mother.

A woman may fear being in a hospital. Underlying her fear is that the main reason she has gone to the hospital to give birth is that she fears something may go wrong with her delivery. The hospital unconsciously reinforces this kind of fear. An intravenous procedure is used for fear of dehydration, "failure to progress," and the need of emergency medication. Electronic fetal monitoring is often used for fear that something may go wrong with the baby during labor; and the delivery room is set up like an operating room for fear that something may go wrong and an operation may be necessary. Those "in case of" practices by the doctor may be interpreted as "for fear that" by the mother. A good childbirth class can help overcome many of the fears that the current medical system has perpetuated.

How a Christian Childbirth Class Functions

In a Christian childbirth class, couples learn all they can about pregnancy, labor, and birth so that fear is no longer an obstacle. The sensations of giving birth are less difficult when the couple understand what is happening and how they can cooperate with the process.

In addition to providing physical and emotional understanding, a Christian childbirth class finds and studies Scripture verses about fear. Meditation on these verses will show that faith is the antidote to the fear. Isaiah 41:10 is a great source of strength: "Fear not, for I am with you; be not dismayed, for I am your God. I will strengthen you, yes, I will help you, I will uphold you with My righteous right hand." Imagine being in labor cradled in the arms of your Father-Creator! As stated in 1 Peter 5:7, you can cast "all your care upon Him, for He cares for you." As you are held by Him in labor, hear Him saying your name, soothing away your fears with the promises of Isaiah 43:1: "Fear not, for I have redeemed you; I have called you by your name; you are Mine."

The message of 1 John 4:18 is definite: "There is no fear in love; but perfect love casts out fear." What greater expression of love is there than giving birth—giving love by bearing what was conceived in love—a new person with whom to share God's love? God wants us to overcome our fears and look to Him, as He said in John 14:27, "Peace I leave with you, My peace I give to you; not as the world gives do I give to you. Let not your heart be troubled, neither let it be afraid." The world makes childbirth a thing to be feared, but Jesus, the author of life, said, "Do not be afraid." First Timothy 2:15 says, "She will be saved in childbearing if they continue in faith, love, and holiness." And 2 Timothy 1:7 says that God did not give us a spirit of timidity (or fear); that spirit comes from Satan.

Fear in childbirth can result in a long line of undesirable effects, even to the point of affecting your total commitment as parents. Mothers who have negative birth experiences have high risks of postpartum adjustment problems. This is one of the main ways Satan defeats the strength and unity of the family.

Your family's birth event needs to be bathed in prayer and faith so that the evil one cannot get you off to a bad start. Faith predominates over fear so that even if you do find yourself confronted by a surgical or medical intervention, you will be able to turn it over to God and proceed in a spirit of faith, not fear. During childbirth preparation, you will learn how to overcome fear and tension together and how to work with the labor process. You will have the best labor support system available—the promises of God. You can look to Him as the Great Physician and rest secure in His care so that childbirth without fear can be a reality.

A Christian childbirth class is led by a qualified childbirth educator. Couples are part of a small, intimate support group that learns and prays together. The series of eight to ten classes starts in the sixth month of pregnancy and meets once a week for about two hours in the comfort of someone's home, if possible. One of the fathers opens each class with prayer, committing their special time together to learning God's plan for each couple in their own childbirth experience. A list of Scripture references provides a study of various topics, such as the ones already mentioned concerning fear and pain. For example, for the discussion of physical conditioning, refer to Proverbs 31:17; Exodus 1:19; 2 Chronicles 15:7. For nutrition, use 3 John 2 and 1 Corinthians 6:19–20. For labor and birth, read Psalms 22:9–10; 71:6; Isaiah 66:7–9. For relaxation, refer to Matthew 11:28–30 and Psalm 37:7. The possibilities of relating Scripture to childbirth are endless and creative. Verses can be copied on index cards to be used during difficult moments of the labor.

During the class, couples share experiences from

their previous births. These can be a great encouragement and lesson for first-timers.

In addition to stressing Christian principles, the classes provide the same basic ingredients of any good childbirth class—exercises, relaxation, breathing, a physiology of pregnancy and birth, comfort measures, information on various medications and procedures, and specific instructions on how the couple can work together (supporting and working with the mother's body). Alternatives of childbirth methods are covered, such as birthing rooms, siblings at birth, bonding, and rooming-in. Nutrition is emphasized, and things to be avoided during pregnancy are discussed.

A good class usually provides a lending library and presents slides or films showing labor, birth, and the surrounding events. Breastfeeding information and discussions of life with a new baby are important. Postpartum adjustment can be a big shock physically and emotionally to first-time parents, so some discussion and sharing in this area are important.

My wife, Martha, taught childbirth preparation for seven years. As a pediatrician, I looked forward once a week to opening up our living room to the joyous instruction of expectant couples. A particular aspect of those Christian childbirth classes I enjoyed is what I call the "show-and-tell" night. A few weeks after every one in the class has delivered, couples and their babies meet for a postnatal discussion class in which they share how beautifully God worked in the miracle of birth. It is also a night of prayer and praise—prayer for any of the new parents who were having postpartum adjustment problems and praise for the new lives God has given them. Eventually, these couples may decide to continue meeting as a support group for Bible study as they progress through the challenges of parenting. A Christian childbirth class is the ideal. If there are none nearby find the best natural childbirth class you can (not always the one taught at the hospital, where often what you learn is how to be a good patient). Supplement this class with the books recommended in the Bibliography. Start reading early to help find the "right" class. (*Childbirth Without Fear, Natural Childbirth and the Christian Family,* and *Under the Apple Tree* are good resource books.)

Couples must take their childbirth class seriously, giving it top priority in their schedules. Getting thoroughly and competently prepared for the birth of a child reaps benefits out of all proportion to the time invested.

■ Choosing a Labor Support Person

The newest and one of the most valuable members of the birth team is a professional labor support person who is a mother herself, often an obstetrical nurse, midwife, or a woman who has had special training helping new mothers have a safe and satisfying birth. A professional labor assistant serves as an anchor, offering emotional support to the laboring mother, giving her encouragement and empowering her to follow the cues of her body. She helps the mother assume the best birthing positions that help her labor progress most efficiently and less painfully.

The professional labor assistant (PLA) acts as a go-between, helping the parents understand ob-

stetrical tests and intervention that may be needed and helping expectant parents understand and be involved in the decisions. The PLA does not displace the father at birth, but rather she takes the pressure off Dad to be the coach and frees him up to do what a man does best—love his wife. New studies have shown that women who employ a PLA at birth have shorter labors that progress more effectively, are less likely to need episiotomy, and are less likely to need a cesarean section. Using the services of this special woman at birth increases the chances of your having the birth experience you want, especially if you have been labeled as having a "high risk" pregnancy. (We prefer the term *high responsibility* pregnancy rather than *high risk* because having a birth that may require special precautions implies that you need to take more responsibility for your birthing decisions.)

Here are some resources that can help you find a PLA in your community.

- National Association of Childbirth Assistance
- Doulas of North America (DONA), 206-324-5440; fax: 206-325-0472 ■

Choosing a Christian Support Group

Some type of support group is helpful for first-time parents just as a good Bible study group is for the beginning Christian. Support groups consist of experienced parents who are prepared to help new parents.

By acting as an extended family, your support group will assist you in making basic decisions early in your pregnancy. It will also help you develop your own parenting philosophy while, at the same time, making you more aware of what resources are available in your community. Look into some of the following support groups early in your pregnancy.

Parenting classes within your local church. Some churches, especially very large congregations, offer Christian parenting classes, such as Apple Tree Family Ministries. (Address: P.O. Box 9883, Fresno, CA 93794-0883.) These classes may be directed to the newly pregnant and first-time parents. If your church does not offer such classes, perhaps they can recommend some in your community.

La Leche League International (LLLI). The LLLI is perhaps the largest mothers' organization in the world. It was organized by a small group of mothers approximately thirty-five years ago for the purpose of promoting breastfeeding education at a time when the majority of mothers did not breastfeed. Although this group does not advertise itself as Christian, many principles held by LLLI are applicable to Christian parents. Monthly meetings are held in the home of a local La Leche League member. Each leader, besides having practical parenting experience, has special training in counseling new mothers about common concerns of breastfeeding and child care. She also enjoys access to a lending library, a board of medical consultants, and her own continuing education, which she passes on to you. I would advise you to attend a series of league meetings. Although the LLLI motto is "Good mothering through breastfeeding," you will find that the league's policy is basically "good mothering" in all aspects of parenting. (Address: P.O. Box 4079, Schaumberg, IL 60168. Phone: 1-800-LA-LECHE)

Although seeking out and relying on the support of other Christians will enhance your pregnancy experience, a supportive marriage relationship can be the most important factor in a positive pregnancy and labor.

CHAPTER 2

THE
PREGNANT
COUPLE

The responsibility of a child can bring a higher level of maturity to your marriage relationship; pregnancy can add a finishing touch to your commitment. However, if your marriage is on shaky ground, you may be particularly vulnerable to the unstable emotions of pregnancy. A baby does not usually stabilize a marriage that is built on a weak foundation.

Mutual giving is the hallmark of a fulfilled Christian marriage. In parenting, this giving concept is taken one step farther—you both give to a third person. In some respects, giving to your child is easier than giving to each other because a child is a biological extension of yourselves and is more dependent. In pregnancy, you continue the process of coming out of yourselves and accepting another person.

Throughout your pregnancy you are preparing yourselves for a very important aspect of parenting—having a high level of acceptance of whatever temperament your child is blessed with. When you are aware of and sensitive to each other's needs and how to respond to them during pregnancy, you are making a good preparation for parenting. In order to help you be mutually sensitive to each other's needs as a pregnant husband and wife, look at the many physical, emotional, and spiritual changes that occur during pregnancy and discover how these changes all come together to help you mature into parenting Christians.

The First Trimester

Pregnancy is not just growing a baby; it is growing a relationship, and pregnancy adds a real change to the marriage relationship. The physical changes are obvious, but with each physical change there are accompanying emotional changes due to the effects of the hormones of pregnancy. For example, the hormone prolactin, which causes the mother's breasts to develop in order to nourish the baby, also may cause her to feel more maternal.

Husbands need to be aware that the hormones necessary for the development of the baby also are responsible for the unstable emotions experienced by their pregnant wives. Pregnancy may be considered a developmental stage, much like adolescence, and ambivalent feelings are normal. One minute a pregnant wife may feel like praising the Lord for enabling her to be pregnant, and the next minute she may have an identity crisis: "I am going to be somebody's mother, but what will happen to the 'me' I know now?" She may experience the positive feelings called the "pride of pregnancy," which is the proof of her fertility and a delight in nourishing another life within her own body. Or she may have negative feelings: fear of miscarriage, fear of becoming less attractive to her husband, ambivalence about leaving her present job, or worry about her capabilities as a mother. The more unpleasant the wife's symptoms of pregnancy (for example, morning sickness), the more these negative feelings may increase. The first trimester is a period of acceptance and adjustment for both of you, and most of your prayers should be directed toward these ends.

The Second Trimester

The second trimester is usually a quieter period. The fears of the first trimester and the discomfort of morning sickness and fatigue probably will have lessened. The highlight of this period is feeling your baby move (around sixteen weeks for the mother and twenty weeks for the father). Feeling this life together, mother's hand upon the father's hand and both parents' hands upon the baby, will trigger desire to pray for the life inside. At this point, the father feels there is really a baby in there! Feeling your baby move is often the high point of prayer and praise during your pregnancy.

Dependency feelings run high in the second trimester. The wife may feel an increased dependence on her husband as the protector and provider and often may express her own need to be "mothered" and loved, as he is instructed so beautifully in Ephesians 5:25–29. The husband also will depend upon his wife to nourish the child within her.

Pregnancy is the time for you to share positive and negative feelings about your present and future role changes. Weak communications and a lack of appreciation of the emotional and physical changes during pregnancy can mean the difference between regarding pregnancy as a richly rewarding experience and seeing it as the low point of your marriage.

If, by the beginning of the second trimester, your marriage communication is not on a spiritual level of prayer and praise to God for the life all three of you have created and if you are not mutually sensitive to each other's needs, then you should seek professional counsel. Anticipatory guidance, an effective counseling tool during pregnancy, can help you prepare for many of the reality changes of your pregnancy. Communication problems during pregnancy usually stem from one partner's not being aware of the ambivalent feelings within the other person or of how these feelings are responsible for his or her behavior. With prayer and consultation, pregnancy should be a high point of your communication since there certainly is a lot to talk about.

Marital disharmony contributes to a woman's vulnerability to anxiety and depression during pregnancy. Although some of these ambivalent feelings are normal, extreme depression and anxiety for Christian parents may signify a breakdown in the continuum of God's order for marriage and parenting. God ordained that a marriage have a firm foundation before a child is brought into the relationship. Perhaps much of the depression and anxiety during pregnancy arises from concern for what will happen when a child enters a home that is wobbly because the spiritual foundation is weak. The skills necessary for successful, natural childbirth require that a couple be spiritually in tune.

The Third Trimester

By the third trimester (often sooner, of course) the wife's pregnancy will be showing, obviously, and like most women she will begin to experience tremendous pride in her fullness and in the special status that is given to pregnant women. Offers of help will come from all around. Some of the anxiety levels that were high during the first trimester and low during the second trimester will peak again in the third trimester in anticipation of the time of birth.

In spite of the radiant glow that many pregnant women show, at times they may not feel so radiant. In the third trimester, the wife needs constant reassurance from her husband that he loves her in this "state." Special attention to good grooming, taking care of herself (as in being nice to herself, not just "looking good" for others), will do wonders for her self-image at this stage.

The wife's sexual desires will go up and down throughout pregnancy because of the fluctuations of hormone levels and physical changes in her sexual organs. Toward the end of pregnancy, her diminishing sexual interest will result from both a feeling of awkwardness as a sexual partner and a fear of inducing premature labor. This fear is unfounded if your pregnancy is normal. Pregnancy itself may fulfill sexual needs. Bear in mind that although hormonal changes may be a valid reason for diminished sexual desires, the husband's hormones do not change during pregnancy. Near term the wife may become increasingly aware of her husband's sexual needs and also of her inability to satisfy them. Inventiveness in sexual techniques may be useful at this time. *Making Love During Pregnancy,* by Elisabeth Bing and Libby Colman, is sensitively written and illustrated and especially helpful for first-time expectant couples. Cliff and Joyce Penner's book, *The Gift of Sex: A Christian Guide to Sexual Fulfillment* (Waco, TX: Word, 1981), is a wonderful book to encourage couples at any time during their marriages, especially when one or both of them may be struggling to understand and appreciate the gift of sex, including the spiritual aspects of this union God designed.

The Final Month

In the final month the couple's anticipation level will be high. Insomnia for the wife will be common due to her anticipation and to her inability to assume a comfortable sleeping position. Many women leave their jobs in the final month, although others continue to work until the last minute in order to reduce the anxiety of anticipation.

God has provided most women with a nesting instinct, a quiet time in the final month of pregnancy whereby a mother tunes in to the child inside her and feels that her unborn child is a person within the family. This should be a time of peace and quiet, a time to relax and slow down and begin mothering your unborn child. This is probably an early attachment stage so vital to the continuum of the mother-infant attachment after birth.

Part of the nesting instinct may be a sudden burst of energy to clean the house, prepare the nursery, and have everything just right for your baby. Be careful not to overdo it and wear yourself out. Laboring in an exhausted state is not an advantage.

A word about preparing your nursery. It is more important for a Christian couple to prepare their minds and souls for the coming of their baby than to prepare a room. A refreshing change in priorities that I have noticed throughout the past decade is that expectant couples seem less preoccupied with the properly appointed nursery.

Another refreshing and important change I see in my practice is an increasing understanding and acceptance of the wide range of feelings, positive and negative, both partners experience about being pregnant and becoming parents. It is through understanding and expressing these feelings that couples can fully support each other in the months preceding parenthood.

CHAPTER 3

FEELINGS DURING PREGNANCY

From elation to devastation, anticipation to dread, both partners can experience the gambit of emotions regarding being pregnant and becoming parents. If handled with honest communication and a desire to seek God's will, you can turn all these feelings into opportunities for growth and maturing into the parent God intends you to be. Keys to this process include prayer and renewing your commitment to a God-centered life.

Unwanted Pregnancy

For a variety of personal reasons you may not want to be pregnant, but the wife misses her first period and the question of pregnancy arises. This circumstance is one of the most real opportunities you have as a Christian couple to put God's will before your own. Before you have a pregnancy test to confirm your suspicion, pray that you may joyfully accept God's will in the result of the test. Prepare your minds and hearts to accept joyfully what God has designed for you. It is more meaningful to begin this prayer before you know the results of the test because the immediate feeling you have when you know (either positive or negative) can have a snowballing effect on your attitude during your entire pregnancy and can even affect the self-esteem of the child as he or she grows. Accepting the will of your Creator over your own desires is perhaps the most difficult but the most maturing Christian struggle. Psalm 143 is a good opening prayer for you in this circumstance, especially verse 10: "Teach me to do Your will, / For you are my God; / Your Spirit is good. / Lead me in the land of uprightness." Also, remember who is forming and knitting together this new life in the womb (see Ps. 139:4–8)!

Father's Feelings During Pregnancy

Whereas God has blessed the mother with the privilege of carrying, birthing, and nourishing a baby, as a Christian father, you still play a vital role in the pregnancy, birth, and care of your child. In the previous section the wife's feelings during pregnancy were discussed. They are more appreciated because they are more obvious. The father also will have adjustment problems during pregnancy and often will need as much or even more prayer and consultation than his wife.

One of the earliest feelings the father will have is a pride in his masculinity and his fertility. This can be a normal and healthy pride similar to that felt from any accomplishment. To keep this pride in Christian per-

spective, thank God for your pregnancy and acknowledge Him as the ultimate Creator of life.

As the reality of another mouth to feed sinks in,
the fact of responsibility and the concept of the family
may weigh heavily upon you. In addition to the dependency of the new life-to-be, your wife may show a high
level of dependency on you throughout the pregnancy.
These increased responsibilities may make you question
your ability both to father the baby and "mother" the
mother.

It is unfortunate that in a beautiful family event
such as pregnancy, the subject of money has to be
considered at all. However, economic worries are
among the earliest concerns of the new father. Like
many fathers, you may exaggerate this worry way out
of proportion. You may worry about how you are going
to educate your baby even before the birth.

Some men actually experience pregnancylike symptoms during pregnancy and may show a subconscious
desire to share their wife's physical condition. Other
fathers do not envy pregnancy at all, and they regard
this period as a necessary nuisance toward having a baby.
Husbands, if this is your attitude, you may tend to
focus on your baby's arrival, and subconsciously you
may ignore the pregnancy and, therefore, the mother.
This tendency often will be overruled by your wife's
constant physical and emotional changes that serve as
a reminder of the reality of the family pregnancy.

Toward the end of the pregnancy the husband may
have ambivalent feelings about how the baby will affect
his marital relationship. The following tips may help you
handle these uneasy father feelings during pregnancy.

1. *Take stock of your situation.* As the fetus ma-
tures so will you. As your wife is growing your child,

pregnancy may be a time for you to ripen spiritually and become a more mature man. Pregnancy can be inventory time in the fathering business: a time to sit back and define your priorities. It is a time to account for where you have been and where you are going. Specifically, take a hard look at how you are walking with God and how you are walking with your wife. Is your marital relationship God-centered? This is a prerequisite for God-centered parenting. Are you sensitive to your wife's needs during the family pregnancy? As described in Ephesians 5:25, one of the greatest ways you can prepare yourself for loving your child is to continue loving the mother. Does your current job assume priority over your marital relationship? It is important to put your marriage before your job at this stage so that later you can put your fathering before your job.

2. *Get involved in the pregnancy.* The earlier you are involved in the family pregnancy, the more involved you will be throughout the pregnancy and the years of child rearing to come. Involve yourself with the choices you and your wife will make early in your pregnancy: which doctor, which pediatrician, which birthing environment, and so on. Accompany your wife on her visits to the obstetrician or midwife. Involvement increases knowledge of what is going on, and knowledge increases comfort and may therefore result in your shying away less from these many decisions.

3. *Attend Christian childbirth classes.* Father involvement in the childbirth event is one of the major focuses in these classes. In many instances, I feel that the fathers actually benefit as much as or more than the mothers.

4. *Help prepare the nest.* Assist your wife in the tasks of getting ready for the baby, such as going on shopping trips and preparing and decorating the nursery (if you have one). A word of advice: respect your wife's nesting instinct. If major changes in your lifestyle, such as moving to a new house or changing jobs, are necessary, do not make these changes in the last couple of months of pregnancy or too soon after the birth.

5. *Pray daily that God will show you the wisdom to be a father* as He designed fatherhood and to be a husband according to His order for a husband. Read the following Scripture verses during your pregnancy to help you overcome your uneasy father feelings and to prepare you for being a Christian father: Ephesians 5:25; 6:4; Colossians 3:19, 21; Philippians 4:19. Successfully handling these father feelings and becoming a God-centered Christian father during pregnancy will lay the foundation for you to become an effective Christian father when your child arrives.

I pray that God will prepare your heart and soul for the arrival of the new life He has entrusted to your care and for whom He will hold you accountable. What a beautiful sensation you will have if you operate from this level of involvement with your wife and with your God during the time of pregnancy. The deep feeling of involvement will carry over into your commitment to your wife as her spouse and to your child as his or her father, and this commitment will be the foundation from which all future fathering will spring forth.

Prayer and Pregnancy

A custom we have enjoyed as a pregnant couple is the nightly prayer ritual of laying our hands upon the pregnant womb. Our prayer would go something like this: "Father, we thank You for giving us the tiny life within this womb. We acknowledge You as the architect of our developing child. Watch over every dividing cell, every organ, every system as the child You are building nears completion. Into Your hands we commit our child." (Psalm 139:13–16 is a beautiful prayer to use during pregnancy.)

You might also extend this prayer ritual. In addition to praying for the health of your unborn child, pray daily for your own health and the health of your marriage. This daily prayer, beginning early in pregnancy, gets Christian parenthood off to the right start. By inviting God's protection, you are claiming the promises of God in 1 Timothy 2:15: "She will be saved in childbearing if they [husband and wife] continue in faith, love, and holiness, with self-control." Talking to your child in the womb and praying daily for him or her acknowledges that your fetus is already a member of your family to be prayed for. Prayer during pregnancy sets the stage for the moment of birth when you truly can thank God for answering your prayers. Francis and Judith MacNutt have written a unique book entitled *Praying for Your Unborn Child: How Parents' Prayers Can Make a Difference in the Health and Happiness of Their Children* (see Bibliography for a more complete description).

This daily pregnancy prayer and the ritual of laying your hands on the womb may be the father's first act as the spiritual leader of the family and his first step toward a strong father involvement. In our family, this nightly ritual for our preborn baby became such a habit that after her birth I couldn't get to sleep without first laying my hands on our newborn's head and praying for her. I was already hooked! This attachment had begun *in utero*.

Commitment to a God-Centered Life

The most important step toward successful Christian parenting is defining sincerely your degree of *commitment* to being a Christian parent. Dwell upon this for a moment because, unless your commitment is uncompromising, you may have an unfruitful struggle.

Throughout this book, Deuteronomy 6:5–9 will be the master verse for this commitment.

> *You shall love the LORD your God with all your heart, with all your soul, and with all your strength. And these words which I command you today shall be in your heart. You shall teach them diligently to your children, and shall talk of them when you sit in your house, when you walk by the way, when you lie down, and when you rise up. You shall bind them as a sign on your hand, and they shall be as frontlets between your eyes. You shall write them on the doorposts of your house and on your gates.*

The most important ingredient in any relationship is commitment. The more you are committed to making a relationship work, the more successful the relationship will be. Parenting is a relationship between parent and child. It is the strongest of all human bonds. One of the joys of being a pediatrician is seeing how strongly most parents are committed to their children. This commitment is strong because your love for your children is strong. Loving your children is easy because you know them so well. For most parents, commitment to God does not come as easily as commitment to their children because their love of Him is weak and their knowledge of Him is scanty. Knowledge of a person helps the commitment to that person. This was illustrated very simply by our four-year-old daughter, Hayden, who one day said, "The reason children love Mommy and Daddy more than God is because they know Mommy and Daddy better than God."

God anticipated the difficulty parents would have making a full commitment to Him; He knew that you would need help loving and knowing Him and rearing your children according to His plan. For this reason He gave you specific details of what He wants, what you should do, and what your children will become if you follow His instructions. He gave you His Word, or what I call a "Manufacturer's Handbook," to accompany the child that He and you have made. This Handbook is like the owner's manual that often accompanies a car, telling how to start it up and what fuel it needs and giving a regular maintenance schedule for years of trouble-free driving—if the manufacturer's instructions are followed. The manufacturer also admonishes you to expect failure if these instructions are not followed.

The Bible is God's timeless Handbook for parents. It is the inspired Word of God talking to us through the men He chose to write His Book. In it God told people to make personal commitments to Jesus as Lord and Savior. "I am the vine, you are the branches. He who abides in Me, and I in him, bears much fruit; for without Me you can do nothing" (John 15:5). Having committed yourselves to God and to your children, you must examine what He expects of you as parents. Deuteronomy and Proverbs outline the basic instructions that you are to follow.

1. To love God (Deut. 6:5)
2. To fear Him (Deut. 10:12)
3. To walk in His ways, to be an example (Deut. 10:12)
4. To know Him, to have a knowledge and an application of His Word (Deut. 10:13)
5. To teach His Word to your children (Deut. 6:7; 11:19)
6. To discipline your children (Prov. 19:18)
7. To avoid provoking your children to anger (Eph. 6:4)

In this sequence of God's communication to parents, one clear message emerges: before you can instruct your children, you must understand His Word yourselves. First you must know, love, and fear God and live according to His teaching. Then you can impart these concepts to your children.

To Love God

It is significant that God's first message to parents, and the message occurring most frequently in the Old and New Testaments, is to love Him. In any person-to-person relationship where there is genuine love, all else automatically follows.

There are three Greek words for love: *eros,* meaning "passionate love"; *phileo,* meaning "demonstrated natural affection"; and *agape,* meaning an "unconditional love." Most of the time when the word *love* is mentioned in the Bible's Greek text, it is agape love, which is the love God expects from Christians. Agape love takes you out of your preoccupation with yourself and into a commitment with others. When the text uses *phileo,* it means it is not enough to love your child

45

unconditionally. You must express your love to the child in a way that he or she can experience being loved, through the things you say and do to and for that child every day.

I tell parents that the best way for a child to learn agape and phileo love is to witness it being expressed by his or her parents. The same concept holds true in helping your child love God. If he or she sees true love between you as parents, and between you and God, your child has a head start toward a relationship with God. Parents, remember that a child sees what you do, not how you feel. How you show signs of your commitment is more meaningful to a child than what you say or what you feel.

Before reading any farther, take a few minutes to dwell upon your commitment to God, for this is the basis from which all parenting begins. Consider the message of John 3:16: "For God so loved the world that He gave His only begotten Son, that whoever believes in Him should not perish but have everlasting life."

To Fear the Lord

God tells us to fear Him: "What does the LORD your God require of you, but to fear the LORD your God" (Deut. 10:12). The concepts of love and fear coexist inseparably throughout the Bible. The term *fear* in the Bible implies an awesome respect for the power and wisdom of God. In the book of Proverbs (perhaps the best child psychology book ever written), Solomon said that "the fear of the LORD is the beginning of knowledge" (Prov. 1:7). As a Christian parent, when I think about this concept of the fear of the Lord, the first thought I have is of my accountability to God for rearing my children according to His plan (Matt. 18:6; Rom. 14:12; 2 Cor. 5:10). I urge you, parents, to keep this concept of accountability always before you. Dwell upon it by the day, by the hour; think about it as you go to bed and as you get up. Fathers, you especially must have a constant awareness of your accountability to your Father that you are to be the effective spiritual leaders in your families. I sincerely feel that if a home is without spiritual leadership, the father will be called on the carpet first.

To Walk in His Ways and Know Him

After God tells you to love Him and fear Him, He says you should "walk in all His ways" (Deut. 10:12 NIV). Then He adds: "with all your heart and with all your soul" (Deut. 10:12 NIV). He says further, "Fix these words of mine in your hearts and minds; tie them as symbols on your hands and bind them on your foreheads" (Deut. 11:18 NIV). These passages are the earliest and clearest messages that God does not want lukewarm Christian parents. There is an underlying depth of commitment to this message. Your love and fear of Him should be more than superficial lip service, but should be a knowing of Him in your innermost being, an inner commitment that dictates your daily living.

To Teach Your Children

In the passages in Deuteronomy, God follows His main theme of parenting: "Teach them to your children . . . impress them on your children" (Deut. 11:19; 6:7 NIV). These verses are some of the earliest and most compelling biblical mandates to parents to teach their children. They tell parents not only *to* teach but *how* to teach.

Saturate your child's environment with His words, "Talk about them when you sit at home and when you walk along the road, when you lie down and when you get up. Tie them as symbols on your hands and bind them on your foreheads. Write them on the doorframes of your houses and on your gates" (Deut. 6:7–9 NIV). In case you are a slow learner, God gives this message twice—in Deuteronomy 6:5–9 and 11:18–20. Christian parents should read these passages over and over again and attach them to their foreheads and to their doorposts. These are verses of commitment. It is clear that God expects more than Sunday-only Christian teaching. Not only are you to know God's commandments, but you are to obey them.

These passages in Deuteronomy also tell parents to teach by example, giving your children models to observe rather than commandments to obey. You must show your children that you are walking in the way of the Lord by saturating your environment with His teachings. Parents are always on stage in front of their children—a fact that makes their accountability for Christian living an awesome responsibility.

But your witness is not limited to your children. You are told to "write them on the doorposts of *your* house and on *your* gates." It seems that God is laying down specific guidelines for Christian families; they are to be examples to all who enter their homes. There should be no doubt who is the central figure in your household. We have a sign in our home that reads: "As for me and my house, we will serve the LORD" (Josh. 24:15).

To Discipline Your Children

In addition to telling you to teach your children His Word, God tells you to discipline them: "Discipline your son, for in that there is hope" (Prov. 19:18 NIV). *Teach* and *discipline* are similar terms, but as used in the Bible, they differ in degree. Discipline implies more than teaching God's Word to your children. Discipline means training their inner behavior and modifying their tendencies so that they are guided by inner rules that give them direction.

In His book of Proverbs, spoken through Solomon, God emphatically tells you how to discipline your children and what kind of inner rules to impart. Proverbs is the best portion of God's Handbook for parents who wish to discipline their children according to God's plan.

In Proverbs, God gives the same message He gives in Deuteronomy: before parents can impart wisdom and discipline to their children, they must be wise and disciplined themselves. In Proverbs the central theme of Deuteronomy is repeated: "The fear of the LORD is the beginning of knowledge" (Prov. 1:7) and "of wisdom" (Prov. 9:10). In order to discipline your children effectively, you must first fear the Lord and discipline yourself to overcome your inner tendencies toward evil and then fill yourself with Christ-centered living. In this way your children will see that those in charge, their parents, are disciplined according to God's plan. They will rebel against having something imposed on them that their parents are unwilling to accept for themselves.

An important concept for you to derive from the study of Proverbs is the continuum concept of

Christian parenting. (*Continuum* means "a series of interrelated steps, a chain of events.") Proverbs 22:6 is called the master verse of discipline: "Train up a child in the way he should go, / And when he is old he will not depart from it." A child who is disciplined according to Proverbs will most likely impart the same discipline to his or her own children and so on throughout the continuum of successive generations, for "a good man leaves an inheritance to his children's children" (Prov. 13:22). Parents will therefore be held accountable for a long-standing Christian heritage, or lack of it, to their grandchildren, great-grandchildren, and beyond.

The practical application of these principles begins the moment your baby is conceived and continues daily as you seek to honor God and nurture your unborn child with the choices you make that impact your child's health and well-being.

CHAPTER 4

MOTHERING YOUR PREBORN CHILD

■ Mothering, the act of nurturing and caring for your child, begins at the moment of conception. With each bite of food, each glass of water, and each unhealthy substance avoided, you are fostering the health of your child and beginning your journey as a parent. Although not as rigorous as after the baby's birth, the attentive parenting you practice now can greatly influence your child's emotional and physical well-being for years to come.

Nutrition During Pregnancy

Feeding the baby begins even before conception. Good prenatal nutrition, or the lack of it, can affect the development of the fetus profoundly. What you eat is more important than how much you eat. The main nutritional requirements for all growing persons (in this case, mother and fetus) are proteins (at least seventy-five grams per day), calories (approximately five hundred extra), vitamins, and iron.

■ Daily Nutritional Needs

During your pregnancy, each day try to eat the following balanced diet from the five basic food groups:

- *Vegetables.* Three to five servings. (One serving = one cup of raw or a half cup cooked.)
- *Grains (bread, cereal, and pasta).* Five servings. Use whole grains. Avoid grains labeled *enriched* or *bleached,* in which many of the valuable nutrients have been depleted by processing. (One serving = one slice of bread, a half cup cereal or pasta.)
- *Fruits.* Two to four servings. (One serving = a half cup of fruit or one cup of juice.) Use fresh fruit and freshly squeezed juice when possible.
- *Dairy products.* Four servings. (One serving = one cup of milk, a half cup of cottage cheese, yogurt, ice cream, or one ounce of cheese.) If allergic to dairy products, alternative sources of calcium are chickpeas, spinach, kale, refried beans, figs, almond butter, and dried beans. Many mothers who are allergic to milk as a beverage are not allergic to yogurt and some cheeses.
- *Meat, poultry, fish, eggs, and legumes.* Three to four servings. (One serving = three ounces of meat, fish, or poultry, two large eggs, two tablespoons of peanut butter, a cup of cooked legumes, such as beans.)

To make every calorie count, eat nutrient-dense foods, those that pack a lot of nourishment into each calorie. Examples of nutrient-dense foods are lowfat yogurt, eggs, fish, beans, avocados, whole grains, tofu, and turkey. ■

What is a normal weight gain during pregnancy? This varies from woman to woman, but there are some general guidelines. At one time, when "not looking pregnant" was fashionable, strict limits were placed on weight gain. Providing you eat the right foods, such limits are not necessary. The usual, or normal, weight gain during pregnancy is about twenty-four to thirty pounds, and this is distributed as follows:

■ Weight of baby—7½ pounds
■ Weight of placenta—1½ pounds
■ Weight of uterus—3½ pounds
■ Weight of amniotic fluid—2½ pounds
■ Weight of extra blood volume and fluids—8½ pounds or more
■ Weight of breasts—1 pound

A general guide for weight gain during pregnancy is three pounds during the first trimester and about three to four pounds per month thereafter. If underweight to begin with, a woman may show a larger weight gain, adding catch-up pounds early in her pregnancy. This is the body's message that she needs more. Weight gain is an individual situation that should not be legislated by anything except good nutrition. If you are overweight, pregnancy is not the time to try to diet and come out closer to your ideal weight after you give birth. The above nutrition plan should be followed in order to nourish your preborn child properly.

It is unlikely for an expectant mother to put on too much weight by indulging in the foods suggested here. Most women gain excessive weight because they eat the wrong kinds of foods. Avoid junk food and excess salt. It is good to nibble on nutritious snacks between meals. Do not skip meals, and above all, *avoid crash diets* during pregnancy. Poor nutrition can cause low birth weight and premature babies. Your appetite and food consumption should parallel your pregnancy. During the last three months of pregnancy you may be consuming an extra five hundred nutritious calories a day without abnormal weight gain. You may be subject to certain cravings, many of which are high in carbohydrates and are not high in nutritious proteins. You do deserve to pamper yourself occasionally, but it is not wise to overindulge. If you feel well, eat mostly nutritious foods, and show no evidence of abnormal water retention, a restriction of your weight gain should not be necessary.

What to Avoid During Pregnancy

Certain chemicals called "teratogens" are known to cause defects in the fetus. Only a few drugs have absolutely proven to be teratogenic; however, knowledge of the subtle teratogenic effects of some drugs is incomplete. This dilemma is called the "threshold effect." This means that no one knows if a teratogen that harms the fetus extensively will harm it less in smaller doses. It is also possible that very low levels of teratogens may cause very subtle malformations that are difficult to identify. An example of a teratogen that has this threshold effect is alcohol. It is known that a lot of alcohol harms the fetus a lot, but it is not known whether a little alcohol harms the fetus a little.

1. *Alcohol.* "You shall conceive and bear a son. Now therefore, please be careful not to drink wine or similar drink" (Judg. 13:3–4). Recently, experts have recognized that alcohol is one of the most potentially harmful drugs during pregnancy. Excessive alcohol consumption during pregnancy can cause a large spectrum of abnormalities called "fetal alcohol syndrome"—small baby, unusual facial features, and mental retardation. Nearly every organ may be potentially affected by alcohol in the fetal blood, and the greater the alcohol consumption, the greater the severity of the fetal malformations.

How much alcohol can you drink without causing damage to your fetus? As has been established, the threshold effect of teratogens is not known. It is known that five or more drinks at one time or an average of two drinks per day throughout pregnancy can harm your fetus. The term *drink* is defined here as one ounce of alcohol (hard liquor, such as whiskey), one twelve-ounce glass of beer, or one eight-ounce glass of wine. Because no one knows the exact threshold effect of alcohol, it seems wise not to drink any alcohol during pregnancy. Unfortunately, many heavy drinkers are also heavy smokers. This can be a disastrous combination for the fetus.

2. *Nicotine.* Do not smoke during pregnancy. Do *not* compromise. Nicotine decreases the blood supply to your placenta and therefore to your baby. Your smoking can cause your baby to be premature, to have diminished brain growth, and to be smaller than normal; this risk increases in proportion to the number of cigarettes you smoke each day.

3. *Drugs*. When you take a drug, your fetus also takes the drug. For this reason, you should pray and seek professional medical advice before taking a drug, even an over-the-counter drug. The drug is more likely to harm the fetus because he is a rapidly developing organism with limited capabilities to get rid of the drug.

An example of a harmful drug is marijuana. At this writing, marijuana has no *proven* detrimental effects on the fetus. It is known, however, that marijuana can damage brain cells and reproductive cells in experimental animals and probably also in humans. Common sense should dictate that it would be risky to smoke marijuana during pregnancy. Cocaine is a drug that has been proven to be definitely harmful to the preborn baby.

Sometimes a potentially harmful drug is taken during the first month of pregnancy before a woman knows she is pregnant. This is the time of highest risk to the fetus. Before you take even an over-the-counter medication for a suspected "flu," consider whether your symptoms could be due to pregnancy. It would be wise not to take any remedies, such as aspirin or nasal sprays, without first consulting your physician or being sure you are not pregnant. During pregnancy, unless directed so by your physician, refrain from taking any drugs (stimulants, depressants, and others) that alter your bodily functions to an unnatural state.

4. *Caffeine*. At this writing, it is uncertain whether caffeine is harmful to the human fetus. However, caffeine that has been given in very large doses to experimental animals may result in malformation in their fetuses. Until this caffeine question is settled, the

Food and Drug Administration advises pregnant women to limit their consumption of products containing caffeine as a precautionary measure. In order of highest caffeine content, these are coffee, cola, tea, and chocolate. Some over-the-counter pain and cold remedies also contain caffeine; their labels usually identify their content.

It is interesting how God designed the human body to care for itself by sending out warning signals. During pregnancy, many mothers have a natural distaste for cigarettes, alcohol, and caffeine.

Prenatal Bonding

Throughout this book, the concept of harmony with your baby will continually be stressed as one of the most important aspects of God's design. This harmony begins during pregnancy. A new and exciting field of research is concerned with fetal awareness, which means that the emotional state of the mother during the last three months of pregnancy may affect the emotional development of the baby. It is an awesome responsibility to consider that the emotional state during pregnancy can influence the baby's personality.

Recent research has shown that when a pregnant mother becomes anxious or stressed, her stress hormones (adrenaline and cortisone) are increased. These increased hormones cross the placenta into the fetal circulatory system and may cause the baby to be agitated. The hypothesis is that an agitated baby is a disturbed baby. A mother and her preborn baby become a hormonal communication unit. When mother is upset, baby is upset. Constant exposure of the baby's developing brain to stress hormones may result in an overcharged nervous system, later resulting in an emotionally disturbed infant. This may account for the common statement made by parents of a hypersensitive baby, "He came wired that way."

You may create a peaceful womb experience by following these suggestions.

1. *Resolve stress promptly.* Most mothers experience some stress during pregnancy because of their normal ambivalent feelings and because of so many changes that happen so fast. How quickly and effectively you deal with this stress is the important issue. Researchers in fetal awareness believe that temporary stresses do not appear to have any lasting effects on the fetus. Chronic, unresolved conflicts and anxiety throughout most of the final months of pregnancy are most likely to disturb the baby. Keep in mind that you and your baby may share your emotions.

2. *Talk and sing to your baby.* Give your baby pleasant womb memories. Studies have shown that infants later recall the familiar voices that talked and sang to them *in utero*. Newborns were better able to attend to their fathers' voices if they had talked to them before birth, and children were able to learn songs more easily that their mothers had sung to them in the womb.

3. *Play harmonious, calming music.* Preborn babies are calmed by soothing music such as Vivaldi, Mozart, and classical guitar, but they are agitated by rock music. Professional musicians relate they could learn more easily the musical instruments their mothers played during pregnancy (see *The Secret Life of the Unborn Child,* by Thomas Verny and John Kelly, Summit Books, 1981).

4. *Encourage your husband's active involvement.* How your husband feels about you and the baby during pregnancy is an important contributing factor to your emotional harmony. Studies have demonstrated that the fetus becomes very agitated during periods of husband-wife conflict.

5. *Pray for your baby as discussed previously.* I can't help feeling that your baby inside you senses the commitment that awaits him after birth. The following suggested Scripture verses will help you encourage a peaceful womb environment and harmonize your emotions during particularly stressful times.

Isaiah 41:10	1 Peter 5:7
John 14:27	Psalm 71:6
Isaiah 66:9	Philippians 4:6–7
1 Timothy 2:15	Matthew 11:28–30
Psalm 37:4–5	1 John 4:18
Psalm 22:9–10	Proverbs 3:5
Psalm 127:3	Proverbs 17:22
Psalm 4:1	Psalm 139:13–16

How a baby in the womb also senses joyful emotions is beautifully illustrated in Luke 1:44. When Mary greeted Elizabeth, "the babe leaped in [her] womb for joy."

In addition to the preparation for baby described in this chapter, you will need to attend to some more practical matters including selecting and gathering baby gear. As with all aspects of parenting, I believe that the choices you make for where your baby will sleep and what equipment you choose to purchase for your child can enhance the parent-child relationship and be honoring to God.

CHAPTER 5

YOUR BABY'S BELONGINGS

■ Parents are often preoccupied with the preparation of their baby's room; they take a lot of time and go to great expense to fix it the way they want it. Perhaps the least important factor in caring for an infant is having her room equipped with all the latest baby paraphernalia because God has endowed mothers with the most important things needed to care for babies: arms, hands, breasts, eyes. It is more important to spend time and money preparing yourselves than fixing up a room.

Cradles and Rocking Chairs

Babies are accustomed to motion. They have been moving around for nine months. If you choose to have a separate sleeping place for your baby, I advise using a cradle instead of a crib, at least for the first six months. When your baby shifts his weight, the cradle will sway and often lull him to sleep. Many mothers find that they themselves become the newborns' "cradles."

Many babies have to be put to sleep before they are put down, rather than put down to go to sleep. A mother who had been her baby's human cradle for many months told me a humorous story: "I was standing at a party, holding a glass of ginger ale and swaying back and forth from the habit of rocking my baby, when a friend came up to me and asked if I had had too much to drink." The human cradle wears out after a while so rocking chairs are a real must. A rocking chair is probably the most useful gift for a new mother, but before purchasing one, try it out. Be sure the arms are low enough to support the mother's arms comfortably while nursing. The breast and the rocking chair are a winning combination for mothering a baby to sleep. A currently popular, and extremely comfortable, version of the rocking chair is the glider. Though more expensive than traditional rocking chairs, the glider is specially designed to support the mother while breastfeeding and is a welcome place for the hours inevitably spent rocking and nursing your child.

Slings, Swings, and Other Things

I advise parents to use a sling-type carrier such as *The Original Baby Sling* to "wear" their babies on their chests or hips. I have personally studied the effects of babywearing: it makes life easier for the parents and keeps babies more content. Baby carriers bring your baby much closer to you than plastic infant seats and baby buggies. Plastic infant seats were originally designed for sick babies with heart problems who needed to be kept upright. They were not designed to be a substitute for a parent's arms. Although they are useful for some modes of travel and some activities (such as eating in a restaurant with a small infant), they are certainly second best to a sling or front/back carrier.

Windup baby swings are often useful for soothing the fussy baby when the "human swing" wears out. Babies more than three months old usually have enough head control to adapt to the swing, or their heads can be propped up with rolled towels. Mobiles to watch and rattles to grab are good toys to occupy and stimulate babies.

Tiny babies are more attracted to the colors of red and yellow, and they like light and dark contrasts such as black-and-white patterns on cards. Use the marvels of nature to attract and hold your baby's interest. Place your baby in front of a window facing a garden, trees, rain, or anything that is moving. These are God's mobiles and they are usually enjoyed by the curious infant.

Before you bring your baby home from the hospital, you will need to prepare his layette. The following chart will help you know what kinds of items and how much of them to supply.

Supplies

- mild bath soap and shampoo
- mild laundry soap
- diaper pins (if using cloth diapers) 3 pairs
- diaper pail
- rectal thermometer
- cotton balls
- baby bathtub or molded bath aid
- diaper cream, zinc oxide
- cotton-tipped applicators

- rubbing alcohol
- petroleum jelly
- nasal aspirator with 2-inch bulb
- 8 oz. bottles for formula
- 4 oz. bottles for water
- bottle brush

Equipment

- bassinet, cradle, crib
- storage chest for clothing
- infant carseat
- babysling
- changing table or padded work area
- portable bed
- diaper bag
- rocking chair
- vaporizer-humidifier
- night-light

Linens

- flannel-backed rubber pads 4
- crib or bassinet sheets 2
- wash cloth 3
- baby blanket 2–4
- hooded baby towels 2

Clothing

- diapers (cloth) 3 dozen
- diapers (disposable)
- plastic pants (loose-fitting) 4
- receiving blanket 6
- lightweight tops (saques and/or kimonos) 8

- terrycloth sleepers and/or heavyweight saques 8
- booties 3 pairs
- sun hats 2
- warm hats 2
- sweaters 2
- undershirts (3–6 month size) 6
- socks 2 pairs

Part 2

Labor
and
Delivery

CHAPTER 6

THE BIRTH OF A CHRISTIAN FAMILY

The long-anticipated event is near, and you are beginning labor. You are excited and well prepared. With strength from God you have developed the confidence that you will be able to cope with the work of labor and delivery. The childbirth classes you have taken prepared your mind and body to accept the child that God will give you, as well as the type of labor and delivery necessary to birth the child. Many couples prepare themselves for the ideal delivery, and when medical complications necessitate a departure from the "natural" way, they are disappointed. "I feel like a failure," one mother who needed a cesarean section confided in me.

As your labor begins, pray a prayer of acceptance asking God to give you the strength to cope with whatever type of labor and delivery you are blessed with. Ask for the flexibility to accept your doctor's judgment should a medical complication occur that necessitates a departure from the type of delivery you are anticipating.

The length, severity, and characteristics of labor vary greatly from woman to woman and even from one labor to the next for the same woman. The following description of a labor and delivery is a compilation of several labor reports sent to Martha and me from couples who have taken our childbirth classes. It is meant to illustrate how couples rely on the strength of the Lord during this momentous event: "Behold, children are a heritage from the LORD, / The fruit of the womb is a reward" (Ps. 127:3).

Anne wondered what it would be like. The instructor in the childbirth class had said there was no way to describe accurately the sensation of labor to a first-time mother because no two women experience exactly the same thing. Only after she had had a baby would she know fully what the term *labor* entails. Even then, each birth would be different, although her first probably would be the hardest.

Anne had sat wide-eyed through all the classes, gleaning all the information she could get from those who had been through it before. She felt as prepared as she had ever been for anything, and yet in a way she felt totally in the dark. No one had been able to tell her exactly what would happen, how she would react, or what her own experience of labor would be. This caused her to be anxious and fearful, but then she recalled God's Word on the subject: "Be anxious for nothing, but in everything by prayer and supplication, with thanksgiving, let your requests be made known to God" (Phil. 4:6). Giving control to God kept her from building up a lot of fear, and it strengthened her faith in God's ability to do His part. It also helped with her relaxation training.

Anne's last visit to the doctor confirmed that all was well and that the baby really could come any time. Actually her due date had already passed, and she was grateful she hadn't let herself become impatient as the day came and went. She was getting rather uncomfortable with her bulkiness, but she knew that babies are born in God's own time and that He knew the exact hour and minute her little one would be ready. In a way it seemed incredible that the time had gone so quickly. It seemed such a short time ago that the nurse was telling her the pregnancy test was positive; she could still feel the joy that swept over her when she heard the news. And now her baby was nearly ready to be born.

Her baby? She didn't often slip into the singular possessive, because, of course, this was their baby, hers and Bob's. He was already a good father, going to childbirth class, helping her practice, indulging her needs, and best of all, praying for the baby. Just tonight as they had lain in bed praying together, Bob placed his hand on her bulging abdomen, right where they could feel the little feet kicking, and asked the Lord's continued blessing on their child. They watched the baby's movements, so clearly visible in the light from the bedside lamp, and Bob was amazed. They both laughed in agreement when Bob predicted, "That baby is ready."

Little did she know that she would sleep very little that night. She was kept awake by what she thought were Braxton Hicks contractions, which were somehow a bit different from those she had been feeling for months now. The tightenings of her uterus felt more like heavy menstrual cramps, front and back, but without the intensity or discomfort she had imagined she would have in labor. One reason they kept her awake was that she had to get up to go to the bathroom every hour because of the pressure on her bladder. Just as she would get settled and relaxed and would be able to ignore the cramping, it would be necessary to make another trip to the bathroom. This went on all night long, but still she rested and marveled at the goings-on in a pregnant woman's body. It occurred to her that all of this nocturnal activity was good training for when the little one would need her during the night, which would be a lot, if her friends with children were right.

At the 6:00 A.M. trip to the bathroom, Anne had a surprise in store. She found a "bloody show," the red-tinged mucus she had been told to watch for. It was a sign that all those Braxton Hicks (or real labor?) contractions were loosening things up in her cervix, the very early phase of eventually opening up wide enough to let the baby pass through. She knew that this show in itself didn't mean she was in labor, but if the periodic tightenings were to become more regular and pick up in intensity, then this would be it! She tried for some semblance of calm as she slipped back into the bedroom and stood next to Bob who was still sound asleep. She *had* to share this incredible news, but in a way that would assure him she was really fine and that nothing was urgent. Her hand on Bob's shoulder produced a sleepy-eyed greeting that became wide-eyed as she spoke the words, "I think I could be in labor." Anne then shared with Bob the events of the night, and together they wondered what to do next. They prayed for guidance and for the Lord's blessing on what they were about to experience.

Anne decided to take a shower and then, throughout the next couple of hours, alternately walked and lay down, noticing that during the time she was up and about, the contractions were more regular. She was still not sure that she was experiencing labor. She thought, *Labor is supposed to hurt, isn't it? At least like cramps anyway?* And her contractions were painless.

Finally, after Anne had more bloody show, Bob suggested she call the doctor. The doctor advised them to come down to the hospital and be checked. On the way to the hospital, they talked to the Lord. Anne confessed her anxiety and fear of the unknown that lay ahead, and Bob quoted the Scriptures they had prayed over together all through their pregnancy. As Anne heard God's Word from Bob's mouth, she repeated each word and absorbed it fully into her spirit. The knowledge that she was resting in the arms of God gave her the freedom to relax fully and do the deep-sleep breathing she had learned in class. Good thing, too, because all this activity of getting ready and traveling the distance to the hospital was producing more regular contractions. Anne handled them so well that, as Bob told her later, he thought it must be a false alarm.

Entering the Hospital

They arrived at the hospital at 9:00 A.M. and at the words, "I think we're in labor," the receptionist called for a wheelchair. As she and Bob sat waiting to be taken to the labor ward, Anne felt her excitement mounting even more. She was grateful that Bob could be with her and that he would be staying with her the whole time. On the last visit, their doctor had reassured them that hospitals now recognize that a mother responds a whole lot better when her husband is not only allowed but actually encouraged to stay alongside her, providing the support he has learned to give.

Anne felt a bit silly riding in the wheelchair because she certainly didn't consider herself an invalid, and it was not too comfortable to deal with a contraction as she was being pushed along the corridor and into the elevator. She decided that if she had another contraction in the wheelchair, she would ask the nurse to stop for a minute.

But then they were at the labor ward and were being taken to one of the birthing rooms. Anne walked around the pleasant room, admiring the pretty drapes and homey bedspread. She headed straight for the rocking chair and sat in it, thinking that in a matter of hours she would be sitting in it, rocking their newborn baby. Bob turned on the stereo so they could listen to the tapes they had chosen to bring along, the relaxing classical music and the soft inspirational singing that Anne loved so much. Bob was in a silly mood and soon had everyone laughing as he and Anne were introduced to their own nurse who would be with them through the labor and birth. This lighthearted mood was good for Anne, for "a merry heart does good, like medicine" (Prov. 17:22); the joking put her completely at ease, as she would have been if she had been at home.

The nurse helped Anne get into a nightgown and settled comfortably, and then checked her progress. Anne was 80 percent effaced and two centimeters dilated, so they could see that all those contractions, even though painless, were having their effect. Bob and Anne were left alone during the next couple of hours to rest and relax, and they both dozed a bit to make up for their early rising. Now that Anne was completely relaxing, she found the contractions to be less uncomfortable somehow, even though they were coming every five minutes and seemed to exert a lot more pressure.

By 11:30 A.M. Anne was 100 percent effaced and four centimeters dilated. This was wonderful news—it looked like all systems were "go." They had previously agreed with Anne's doctor that if she were not in active labor they would be able to go home till things got moving. As the morning passed into afternoon, the contractions got harder, but using deep-sleep breathing and relaxation, Anne was able to remain fairly comfortable She was able to release her abdominal muscles rather than brace them against the contractions. Bob shared some of the Scripture verses from time to time that Anne had written on three-by-five-inch cards. Anne was especially pleased when she and Bob could pray together, keeping the Lord as involved with the labor as they were.

Anne spent a lot of time moving around the room and occasionally strolled down the hall to have a change of scenery. She felt the contractions were really a lot more comfortable when she was up and about or when she was sitting in the rocker. She remembered to use the bathroom every hour to keep her bladder empty so the baby would have lots of room to move down. This also kept the contractions more comfortable.

By 4:00 P.M. labor had become more intense. Anne felt a lot more serious about things, and Bob found that she stopped midsentence to respond to a contraction with deep breathing and relaxing. He also learned to stop joking around and to pay full attention to her, especially during a contraction, to be sure she kept her limbs, face, abdomen, and pelvis relaxed. So with all this help, even though labor was now very intense, it was still bearable. Bob stayed busy rubbing her back, giving her ice chips and sips of juice, wiping her forehead, and now and then sharing more Scripture verses with her. Sitting in the rocker or on the side of the bed was no longer comfortable, so she stuck to walking around. She occasionally lay down on the bed for a rest, using the side-lying position she had found so comfortable for sleeping in the last months of pregnancy.

The doctor came in to check Anne and said she was seven to eight centimeters dilated. This progress seemed slow, but they thanked God for His timing and for His love and care for them. Only a few minutes after the doctor left the room, Anne's water broke with a gush. The labor suddenly became much harder, more intense, and rather painful, especially in her lower back. Anne and Bob both realized this was because the bag of water was gone, and the cervix was now being wedged open by the hardness of their baby's head.

Anne began to get upset and frightened because she couldn't breathe slowly enough and because she had cried out once when the sensations seemed overwhelming. Bob had been watching for these symptoms that they had learned might occur during transition. Anne was skeptical when he reminded her this phase would soon pass. Bob was really busy now, using counterpressure on her back and breathing slowly and loudly in order to help Anne pace her own rhythm.

Bob appreciated the nurse's presence, who had come in when Bob signaled that the water had broken. The nurse suggested a change in position. They helped Anne into a recliner-chair position by adjusting the bed and putting pillows under her knees to help her relax her legs. Anne was having such an overwhelming sensation of rectal pressure that she began to bear down with one especially strong contraction. So at 5:00 P.M. the nurse checked again and found that she had dilated to nine centimeters. What good news! All this hard stuff *was* the transition phase, and the cervix was nearly completely dilated. Anne was asked not to push until the rim of the cervix could disappear. She found it very hard to obey these instructions because she had such an overwhelming urge to push, so the nurse finally pushed the rim away manually during a contraction. "Now you can push," the nurse said, and Anne was ready.

As the nurse summoned the doctor, Bob helped Anne get upright into a squatting position, reminding her what was needed for proper pushing. When she felt the urge, she would take two full breaths, holding the third breath as she leaned forward into the push with her back rounded, head forward (chin on chest), knees wide apart, and pelvis tilted to curve around so that the birth passage would open to the fullest angle. As Anne bore down evenly, she let her breath out evenly and slowly and then took in another chestful of air. She continued pushing this way until the contraction was gone.

The nurse reminded Anne to relax the "baby door" muscles and reminded her that the strange sensations she had low in her pelvis and perineum were normal birthing sensations and nothing to fear. Anne found that when she followed her body's urge to push hard and long with each contraction, everything felt so good, so right. Even though she had been feeling extremely tired before the pushing started and had wondered how she would manage (she even asked the Lord to give her a little vacation, just skip one contraction), she found a second wind and her energy returned. She thought, *So this is what they meant when they called it labor!* Anne felt her body working harder than it ever had before, yet everything felt right. Even the burning sensation in her perineum didn't unnerve her because the doctor announced that he could see some dark hair about the size of a silver dollar—the baby's head! What a reward for all their labor!

Bob was sent to the bathroom to change into a scrub suit, and, to Anne, he seemed to take forever. She called, "Bob, I need you . . . *now!*" Things seemed to be happening so fast, and Anne felt she could not control the situation alone. Bob hurried back to her side, scrub suit half on, mask and cap dangling untied. With Bob's help to hold on to her legs and the nurse's encouragement to reach down and feel her baby's head, Anne's pushing became effective again, and she worked with the powerful forces in her uterus, feeling the baby advance a bit with each contraction. She heard Bob encourage her with the words of Philippians 4:13: "I can do all things through Christ who strengthens me." She pushed well for two more contractions, resting gratefully in between. Halfway through the next contraction the doctor said, "Don't push . . . breathe." The doctor wanted her to "breathe the baby out" while he supported her perineum and did the maneuvers needed to avoid an episiotomy. This took a lot of concentration on Anne's part because of the incredible pressure. But Bob helped by reminding her to keep her perineal muscles relaxed. He also told her to keep her eyes open so she wouldn't miss the birth.

They watched in awe as the baby's head emerged. Then there was a bit of a rest, and the pressure eased somewhat. They saw their baby's face for the first time as the baby's head turned toward the side and then up as the doctor eased each shoulder free. Anne could not believe the flood of physical and emotional sensations she felt as the baby moved through her body. She actually could feel the baby's chest movements as the baby lingered half in and half out of her body. Anne had waited so long for this moment. She reached down and took hold of the tiny little body, while the doctor used a rubber bulb to suck out the mucus from the baby's mouth. Then she (with the doctor's help) drew him up onto her abdomen. The baby gave two short, strong cries as he deeply breathed in air for the first time. At the same time the doctor exclaimed, "Praise the Lord! You have a boy." Anne stroked his little back and cradled him close to her while the nurse covered him with a warm blanket. Then the baby was quiet, peaceful, and eager to look around, his eyes coming to rest and gazing right into the eyes of his mother.

"David, little David! Oh, Bob, God gave us a son! Thank You, Lord! Thank You!" Anne and Bob both broke forth with prayers of thanksgiving as they drank in the sight of their baby boy with hungry eyes. Anne looked at Bob and saw tears streaming down his face. They shared something at that moment that surprised them both, a surge of love warmer than ever before, and they felt closer to each other and closer to God. The next few hours were spent basking in feelings of closeness and warmth. Everything felt so right, as though it had been specially designed by the Creator for this time of opening up and including little David in their circle of love.

The doctor and nurse quietly finished up their tasks of making sure all was well and seeing to the comfort of the new family. No one interfered with the precious bonding process taking place—the birth of a family. A prayer came through Anne's mind over and over: "Thank You, God, for dealing so bountifully with Bob and me. Oh, heavenly Father, who gives only perfect gifts, You really outdid Yourself when You created David."

This birth description is unique. No birth will be exactly like it, and many will be quite different. This is part of God's creative world. Helen Wessel's first book, *Natural Childbirth and the Christian Family,* is an excellent source for learning more about this miraculous process.

■ Making Progress

To ease the discomfort and help your labor progress more efficiently, imagine PROGRESS.

P: *Prayer and proper position.* **Throughout your labor, pray that God may give you wisdom to listen to the cues of your body and strength to help your labor progress. Adjust your** *positions* **throughout your labor according to the cues of your body. Remember, the position that is most comfortable for you is usually most healthy for baby.**

R: *Relax and release your mind and muscles during labor.* **Take along Scripture verses on 3 x 5 cards. During your slow, deep breathing techniques and while listening to relaxing music, read your Scripture verses, such as Psalm 23:2: "He makes me to lie down in green pastures; / He leads me beside the still waters."**

O: *Output.* A full bladder creates more labor pain. Urinate at least every hour.

G: *Gravity.* Helps your labor progress more efficiently. Be upright and moving as much as possible. Squatting, kneeling, or walking helps move labor along.

R: *Rest* your mind and body between contractions.

E: *Energy.* To avoid dehydration, drink lots of fluids and snack on nutritious, nutrient-dense foods.

S: *Submerge* in water using a labor pool or tub.

S: *Support during labor.* Use a professional labor assistant and the loving touch of your husband. ■

Water—An Excellent Relaxation Tool

Relaxation skills during labor do work to decrease or eliminate pain, but not all women are able to master the art of total body relaxation even during pregnancy. Once labor begins and escalates, the inability to relax takes its toll. Immersion in a warm tub (98 to 100 degrees, body temperature) deep enough to cover the mother's abdomen is a very simple, drug-free method of enabling a tense, laboring woman to fully relax so that her uterus can get on with the work of birth without the obstacles of tension and pain. The buoyancy of the water enables the mother to more easily support her body and relax during the contractions. As she relaxes, her stress hormones decrease and the natural birth-progressing hormones (oxytocin and endorphins) flow uninhibited.

During the labor with our seventh baby, Martha experienced excruciating suprapubic (low front) pain. After trying the all-fours position and other comfort measures without relief, she got into the tub. She was finally able to relax enough and the pain literally melted away. When the birth was imminent she got out of the water to deliver, and then we saw the reason for the unusual pain—the baby's hand came out wedged alongside his head, a compound presentation.

Birthing tubs are intended to be used to ease the pain and improve the progress of labor. Many women actually give birth in the water, and studies show lower rates of infection than in traditional births and no detrimental effects on the baby. (For an in-depth discussion of the benefits, techniques, and safety of water labor and birthing, see the following reference: *Journal of Nurse-Midwifery*, Vol. 34, pp. 165–70, 1989).

CHAPTER 7

THE
FIRST HOUR
AFTER BIRTH

If your labor and delivery have been relatively normal and uncomplicated, the first hour after birth can be a glorious time of bonding with your newborn. *Bonding* is a term used to describe the close physical and emotional attachment between you and your child at the time of birth. Bonding was designed by the Creator to enable you to get to know each other right away. During your pregnancy you began to form a bond with your baby. This bond was strengthened by the constant awareness of the life inside you. The physical and chemical changes occurring in your body reminded you of the presence of this being. After birth, this bond does not stop simply because your baby is no longer a physical part of you. Birth should not break this bond but should further cement it. Birth gives reality to the mother-infant bond. You now can see, feel, and talk to the little person whom before you knew only by the bulge, the movements, and the heartbeat you heard through medical instruments. Bonding allows you to transfer your life-giving love for your inside infant to the caregiving love for your outside infant. Inside, you gave your womb; outside, you give your milk, your eyes, your hands, your voice—your entire self. This continuum of mother-infant attachment should not be interrupted by trivial routines nor diluted by depressant medications.

The first hour after birth is a sensitive period. Unless a medical complication prevents it, your baby should be placed immediately onto your warm, soft abdomen and breasts instead of onto a hard, uncaring surface or into a plastic box. This immediate, postpartum period should be a private time of mutual touching. This initial family time should be spent touching, talking to, and suckling your baby. The first hour after birth is an important milestone for your entire parenting career. It is a special time in which mothers and fathers are very high from the excitement of the birth, and babies are in a state of quiet alertness, the state of awareness in which babies are most receptive to their caregiver. Neither you nor your newborn should be deprived of this special time.

How does this early bonding benefit you and your baby? Medical science is continually trying to prove what mothers have intuitively known and God designed from the beginning. Much of the research on mother-infant bonding was popularized by Doctors Klaus and Kennell in their book, *Parent-Infant Bonding*. These researchers compared two groups of mothering styles: the early-contact group bonded with their babies immediately after birth, and the delayed-contact group were temporarily separated from their babies immediately after birth. They found that the following mothering abilities were greater in the early-contact group: (1) They were more successful at breastfeeding;

(2) they talked with their infants more and used descriptive speech; (3) they spent more time in the face-to-face *(enface)* position of eye-to-eye contact; and (4) they touched and groomed their infants more.

These researchers postulated that there is a sensitive period lasting about one hour after birth when the baby is most sensitive and receptive to his caregiver. Mothers who bonded with their babies during this period were more confident in exercising their intuitive mothering; whereas, the mothers who were separated during this period were less confident. These researchers also found that fathers who were present at birth and who bonded with their babies during this sensitive period continued this involvement and were closer to their children.

What happens in a situation in which a medical complication, such as a cesarean delivery, temporarily separates mother and baby after birth? What happens in cases of adoption? Is this parent-baby relationship permanently affected by a temporary separation, or can you make up for the time you were separated (delayed bonding)? Recent studies have questioned the conclusions that bonding or not bonding during the first hour after birth can have any lasting effects on either parent or child. This is an important point. Parents who are medically unable to bond with their baby immediately after birth should not feel guilty that their child has been permanently affected. Immediate bonding after birth is not like a glue that cements the parent-infant relationship forever. Many steps must be taken throughout infancy and childhood that lead to a strong parent-infant attachment. I feel that there is probably no scientific rationale for concluding that being deprived of this initial bonding can permanently affect the parent or child. I do feel, however, that bonding during this biologically sensitive period does give the entire parent-child relationship a head start. Regardless of whether Klaus and Kennell's studies are scientifically accepted or rejected, it is true that their pioneer work in parent-infant attachment has been a valuable impetus toward changing many hospital policies that have separated parents and newborns after birth.

Bonding Tips

The following suggestions are designed to get you off to the right start and help your bonding relationship be more meaningful.

1. *Be prepared.* A positive birthing experience usually encourages maternal bonding; whereas, a negative birthing experience in which fear and suffering predominate often lessens the desire for a mother to bond with her infant. Two important factors that contribute to a positive birthing experience and, therefore, indirectly promote a positive bonding experience are Christian childbirth classes and a supportive father during labor and delivery.

Pain-lessening drugs given to the mother during labor may decrease the mother's and the baby's receptiveness to the bonding experience. Mothers who have been well prepared for birth by a childbirth class do not require any (or require far fewer) drugs during labor. If for any reasons beyond your control you have had a negative birthing experience in which fear and suffering predominated or medical complications occurred, realize that your feelings of attachment to your baby may be temporarily lessened. This is a time for sincere prayer and consultation, asking God not to allow your feeling of disappointment in the birthing experience to lessen your attachment toward your baby. Pray for healing from this difficult experience.

2. *Breastfeed your baby right after delivery.* Some babies have a strong desire to suckle the breast immediately after birth, and others are content simply to lick the nipple. Medical research clearly demonstrates that babies should be put to the breast immediately after birth. Sucking and licking the nipple release the hormone oxytocin into your bloodstream. The oxytocin increases the contraction of your uterus and lessens the complication of postpartum bleeding. This early suckling also stimulates the release of the hormone prolactin, the milk-producing hormone, which also enhances your mothering abilities after birth. I like to call prolactin the "mothering hormone."

3. *Touch your baby.* Ideally, immediately after birth your baby should be skin to skin on you, his or her chest to your abdomen, with your arms around him or her and a blanket over your arms. The skin is the largest organ of the human body—your newborn will enjoy the stimulation he or she receives from this skin-to-skin contact. Gently stroke your baby, touching his or her whole body. It is moving to see a new mother stroke her baby's entire body with a gentle caress of her fingertips and to see the father place an entire hand on his baby's head as if symbolizing his commitment to protect the life he has fathered.

4. *Look at your baby.* Place your face in the *enface* position so that your eyes and your baby's eyes meet on the same vertical plane. Your newborn can see you at best within the distance of twelve inches. Because they are in a state of quiet alertness after birth, many infants will open their eyes more during the first hour after birth than they will several hours after birth when they are usually in a state of deep sleep. The feedback you will receive by staring into your infant's eyes may trigger a rush of beautiful mothering feelings. Cradling your baby in your arms while breastfeeding lends itself to the *enface* relationship. Request the nurses to delay the eye ointment (given to prevent eye infection) until after the bonding period since this ointment may lessen your baby's ability to open his or her eyes.

5. *Talk to your newborn.* Mothers naturally speak to their newborn babies in high-pitched, mothering voices. Your newborn's ears are already attuned to your speech, and you may notice that your baby moves rhythmically in response to your voice.

6. *Have some private time.* If no medical problems occur, a perceptive hospital staff will leave mother, father, and baby alone for a while after birth. This should be a time of peace and privacy, the birth of a family. It is a time when all three of you should embrace one another. It is a time to acknowledge God's presence in the birthing room (if you haven't already) and to pray a prayer of thanksgiving for the life that He has given you.

Rooming-In

Rooming-in is the natural extension of the bonding period. After birth, both you and your baby will fall into a much-deserved sleep. After the baby's initial hour of alertness, he probably will reward you with two or three hours of deep sleep. For most mothers, the ecstasy of the birth event is eventually overruled by the tiredness of their bodies, and mothers also can enjoy their much-needed, long sleep.

The next attachment decision is, Who will be your baby's primary caregiver in the hospital, you or the nursery staff? Like so many other options that have diluted the parenting profession, there are several options of newborn care, some of which unfortunately may interfere with mother-infant attachment in the hospital. One option of newborn care, which I strongly discourage, is giving the baby's primary care to the nursery staff who bring the baby to the mother on a predetermined schedule or at their convenience. In my opinion, this option should be reserved only for sick mothers or sick babies. Not only does it deprive the mother of caring for the life she nourished for so long, but it is not conducive to early mother-infant attachment. This scheduled newborn care puts the mother in the role of secondary caregiver, a role not at all in accordance with God's design. Hospitals should not consider mothering as a drug for the baby that is to be dispensed in concentrated doses at prescribed times.

A second option, and one many mothers elect, is that of modified rooming-in. In this option the newborn spends most of the day with the mother but spends the night in the nursery and is brought out as needed for night feedings. In theory this modified type of rooming-in seems attractive, and the mother apparently gets the best of both worlds. Actually, this situation often becomes confusing to both mother and baby, and the baby may wind up spending a lot of time in the nursery.

The third option, and the one I strongly encourage, is full rooming-in. In my opinion, healthy mothers and healthy babies should stay together from birth to the time of discharge from the hospital. The nursery should be reserved for sick babies or babies of sick mothers. Full rooming-in will allow you to exercise immediately your intuitive mothering at a time when the hormones in your body are programmed to help you begin your mothering profession. Studies have shown that infants who room in with their mothers cry less and more readily organize their sleep-wake cycles. As a former director of a university hospital newborn nursery I noticed that the mother and baby who fully room in together enjoy the following benefits.

1. The mother has fewer breastfeeding problems. Her milk is established sooner and her infant is more satisfied.
2. The newborn has less jaundice, probably because he or she gets more milk.
3. The mother actually seems to get more rest since she experiences less separation anxiety, and the newborn will sleep most of the time anyway.
4. Babies in a large nursery are soothed by tape recordings of a human heartbeat. Rather than being soothed electronically, the baby who is fully rooming in with his mother can be soothed by the real thing.
5. The newborn seems more content because he interacts with only one caregiver, his own mother. The rooming-in mother is much more competent and intuitive in the care of her newborn once they get home.
6. Research has shown that the rooming-in mother has a lower incidence of postpartum depression.

Rooming-in truly does allow the best of both worlds, and is, in my opinion, the ideal arrangement. It encourages you to exercise fully your intuitive mothering according to your desires and the needs of your baby rather than the impersonal nursery clock. This arrangement also affords you the luxury of having the attending medical personnel in the roles of adviser and consultant should the need arise. Rooming-in is the natural extension in the continuum of attachment— mother's womb to mother's room.

CHAPTER 8

ROUTINE
HOSPITAL
PROCEDURES

Shortly after your child's birth, several routine
tests and procedures must be performed to continue your newborn's care. Each of the procedures
mentioned is fairly standard and should only take a few
minutes. In some instances, you can ask for the tests to
be delayed so as not to interfere with your parent-child
bonding. Review your hospital's policies on these procedures before your due date and note what excep-
tions or alternatives are allowed and then discuss your
preferences with your obstetrician and your birth
attendant.

Apgar Scoring

Within the first five minutes after birth, your newborn will be given a score called the Apgar score, which
is a measure of the general health of newborn babies
developed by Dr. Virginia Apgar over thirty-five years
ago. The Apgar scoring is performed at one and five
minutes after birth, and your newborn is given from

zero to two points for each of the following parameters: color, breathing efforts, heart rate, muscle tone, and general reflexes. An infant who receives a score of ten has received two points for each of these parameters, indicating that each system was functioning at its maximum; whereas, a score toward the lower end of the scale (four or five) indicates that some of these systems were not functioning at their maximum within the first five minutes after birth.

Since it is often customary to tell the parents the Apgar score, let me explain its real meaning in order to alleviate any anxiety you may have. Infants who are pink all over, cry lustily, breathe rapidly, have good heart rates, and show strong muscle movements are usually given scores of ten. Most of the time, normal, healthy newborns do not achieve scores of ten. It is quite normal for the hands and feet of a newly born baby to be somewhat blue because it takes a few minutes for the newborn's circulatory system to become adjusted to his postnatal environment.

It is a misconception that it is healthy for a newborn to cry lustily after birth. Some newborns are born in a state of quiet alertness. This is a normal state of peace and contentment for which the newborn would lose two points on the Apgar score. A baby who scores ten is not necessarily more healthy than a baby who scores seven or eight. The Apgar score is only valid if done by a trained medical person whose only responsibility in the delivery suite is to calculate that score. The score number given to the parents after birth has little or no predictive value as to the health of the baby. A lower score should not be a source of anxiety to the parents. It only serves to alert the attending medical personnel to observe the baby more closely over the next few hours in case circulatory or respiratory problems occur.

Injections and Medications

Immediately after birth your newborn will be given an injection of vitamin K because most newborns are deficient in this vitamin that enhances normal blood clotting. It is also a law in most states that your baby be given some medication in both eyes in order to prevent any infection of the cornea that may have been picked up during passage through the vaginal canal. Silver nitrate was the solution most commonly used, but this solution may temporarily irritate the eyes. It is now replaced by a milder but equally effective ointment such as erythromycin.

Although these procedures are necessary to ensure the health of your newborn, it is not necessary that they be administered immediately after birth. If you wish to have the special time of bonding and thanksgiving prayers after birth, you can request the attending medical personnel to delay these routine procedures until after you have finished.

PKU Testing

Phenylketonuria (PKU) is an extremely rare metabolic disorder occurring in approximately one out of fifteen thousand infants. If diagnosed shortly after birth, it can be treated with a special diet. If left untreated, it can result in brain damage. The PKU test, required by law in most states, is usually done just prior to discharge from the hospital, and it is conducted on a few drops of your baby's blood. Because of the rarity of this disease, sometimes too much anxiety is produced in the parents by this simple test. I became aware of this when new parents came into my office one day concerned that their baby had missed the "mental retardation test" because they had left the hospital too early. This misunderstanding illustrates the importance of properly explaining hospital procedures to parents.

Thyroid Testing

Your baby's blood is also analyzed for sufficient thyroid hormones. Congenital hypothyroidism (low thyroid at birth) occurs in about one out of five thousand infants and may cause retardation if untreated. The earlier this disease can be detected and treated, the more effective the treatment.

Jaundice

Jaundice is listed under the category of routine hospital procedures and tests because almost all newborns develop some degree of jaundice, and parents often are anxious over what in reality is a variant of a normal physiologic process. Jaundice is the yellow color in a baby's skin caused by a buildup in the blood of a yellow pigment called bilirubin. The body normally produces some bilirubin from the breakdown of worn-out red blood cells. This bilirubin is usually disposed of through our livers and intestines and does not reach high enough levels in the blood to cause yellow deposits in the skin. If too many blood cells are broken up too fast, or if the liver is unable to get rid of the excess bilirubin fast enough, this excess bilirubin is deposited into the skin, giving the yellow color.

Newborns are susceptible to two types of jaundice: (1) normal and (2) abnormal. I use the term *normal jaundice* (also called "physiologic jaundice") because almost all babies have some degree of jaundice. This is due to a series of immaturities within the newborn baby—temporary immaturity of the liver and intestinal mechanisms—to dispose of the bilirubin. Within the first few weeks, your baby's systems mature enough to dispose of the bilirubin, and the jaundice subsides. Your pediatrician will tell you whether your baby's jaundice is normal or whether it is due to some abnormality. Because this normal type of newborn jaundice causes much anxiety in the new mother and is often over-treated, the following is a detailed explanation to alleviate this unnecessary anxiety. Ways also are given in which you can often lessen the level of jaundice in your newborn.

The first concept to understand is that in many cases jaundice is a reflection of the fact that God's design for mother-infant togetherness has been tampered with. As a director of a university hospital newborn nursery, I have noticed that babies who are allowed to room in with their mothers and are breastfed on demand have much less jaundice than those who do not room in and feed frequently. Recent studies have confirmed my observation by showing that the more frequently mothers are allowed to breastfeed babies in the hospital, the lower the bilirubin in their babies. The medical reason for this curious observation is that milk helps wash out the excess bilirubin in the intestines, and infants who do not receive enough milk have fewer calories, which is another cause of jaundice.

Unfortunately, mothers often are advised to stop breastfeeding because the breast milk is assumed to cause the jaundice. A very rare type of this disease called "breast-milk jaundice" is why this treatment is advised. For an unknown reason, the breast milk of some mothers causes prolonged jaundice in a newborn baby. This only occurs in about 1 percent of breastfeeding babies; therefore, it is rarely necessary to stop breastfeeding temporarily when your baby is jaundiced.

There is also an abnormal type of jaundice in which the bilirubin levels may go high enough to cause brain damage in the sick newborn or premature baby. The cause of this type of jaundice is usually blood group incompatibility (such as the Rh factor difference in mother and baby) or an infection. If your baby has jaundice, your doctor will inform you if you should be concerned.

One of the most common modes of treatment of high jaundice is called "phototherapy." Your baby is placed under a bilirubin light that dissolves the bilirubin in the skin, allowing it to be disposed of more adequately through the kidneys.

Regardless of the cause of your baby's jaundice, there is seldom a reason to separate you and your baby. One of the best ways that you can prevent or lessen your baby's jaundice is by keeping your baby with you in the hospital and breastfeeding frequently. Since the jaundice may increase once your baby gets home, your doctor may require that your baby be taken back to the hospital for a follow-up blood test to check the bilirubin level. If it is too high, a home phototherapy light may be required. This explanation is pertinent only for full-term, healthy babies. Premature babies or sick babies at birth follow different rules for the treatment of jaundice, and your doctor will advise you if this is the case. Whatever the cause of your baby's jaundice, it is necessary that both the bilirubin level of the baby and the anxiety level of the parent be appropriately diagnosed and treated.

CHAPTER 9

CARING FOR YOUR NEWBORN

■ While in the hospital you will begin tending to your newborn's basic needs and making decisions about your child's care. If you haven't made up your mind about some of the elective procedures or methods of care before you enter the hospital, you may be unduly swayed by the opinions of the nurse on duty or physician on call. Do as much reading, praying, consulting, and decision making as you can before your child's birth and then make your decisions with the confidence that you are honestly and thoughtfully seeking God's design for your child.

Temperature of Your Baby's Environment

The smaller the baby, the more careful you need to be about changes in temperature. Premature babies and babies weighing less than five pounds may have immature temperature-regulating systems for the first few weeks; therefore they need to be kept warm. Full-term, healthy newborns, especially large ones weighing more than eight pounds, have body fat and mature temperature-regulating systems to adapt easily to an environmental temperature comfortable to an adult. A room temperature of about seventy degrees Fahrenheit is adequate for a full-term, healthy baby. What is more important than the actual temperature is its stability. Babies may not adjust well to marked temperature swings in their first few weeks.

Humidity in the room is important for two reasons: (1) it helps maintain the constancy of the heat, and (2) it keeps your baby's narrow nasal passages from drying out. A relative humidity of at least 50 percent is advisable. A dry climate or your home's central heating may necessitate the use of a humidifier or vaporizer to maintain this humidity. Signs that the humidity in his sleeping room is too low for your baby are persistently clogged nasal passages, snuffling breathing, and dry skin.

Clothing

The way you dress your baby is a matter of culture and temperature. As a general guide, dress your baby in the same amount of clothing you are wearing for a given temperature. Cotton clothing is preferable because it absorbs body moisture and allows air to circulate freely. Also be sure the clothing is loose enough to allow your baby to move freely.

Taking Baby Outside

If you live in a climate where the temperature inside and outside the house is similar, then a full-term baby weighing more than six pounds is able to go outside immediately after birth. By the time your baby weighs about eight pounds, he has enough body fat and his temperature-regulating system is mature enough to tolerate brief exposure to temperature swings, such as those experienced traveling from house to car and back. Babies less than six pounds may not tolerate marked changes in temperature; therefore, it is necessary to maintain some consistency of temperature by traveling from a heated house to a heated car.

Environmental Irritants

Cigarette smoke is the most commonly overlooked irritant to a baby's tiny respiratory passages. Studies have shown that babies of smoking parents have three times the number of respiratory infections found in babies of nonsmoking parents. Persistent nasal stuffiness and hacking coughs are the usual signs of irritation from cigarette smoke. I strongly advise parents to have a strict no-smoking rule in closed spaces such as a house or car, especially around children less than two years old.

■ Clearing Little Noses

Tiny babies have tiny nasal passages. Yet, like older children and adults, babies don't breathe well through their mouth, so they are dependent upon clear nasal passages to breathe comfortably. To help your baby breathe more easily:

■ **Rid your baby's bedroom of nasal irritants, such as fuzzy animals that collect dust,**

cigarette smoke, paint fumes, and aerosols
such as perfume and hairspray.

- Keep your baby away from cigarette smoke.
  Do not allow anyone to smoke in the same
  house as your baby, let alone the same room.
  The respiratory passages of infants and children are particularly injured by the irritating
  effects of cigarette smoke.

- "Hose baby's nose." When your baby's nose
  is stuffy (a clue is she cannot nurse or feed
  comfortably), squirt a drop or two of saltwater nose drops into her nose and gently
  suck out the loosened secretions with a nasal
  aspirator (veteran parents dub this handy gad-
  get a "snot snatcher"). Saltwater nasal sprays
  or drops (called saline) and nasal aspirators
  are available over the counter at pharma-
  cies. ■

Bathing Your Baby

The materials you need to bathe your baby are a
small plastic tub or sponge form, several thick towels,
a pair of white cotton gloves, cotton-tipped applicators,
a mild soap, and an antiseptic solution.

Babies rarely get dirty enough to require a daily
bath for cleanliness. It is usually enough to bathe your
baby totally twice a week and wash her hair no more
than once a week. Wearing cotton gloves will make it
easier for you to hold your slippery baby. Rub some
mild soap on the wet gloves, and use your gloved hands
as a washcloth. Place a towel in the bottom of the
sink or tub to prevent your baby from slipping, or use
specially designed sponge forms. Cotton-tipped applica-

tors are handy for cleaning the creases behind the ears and in the crevices of the navel. After your baby's bath, place her on a soft, padded surface to dry her off.

In reality, bathtime is playtime for both mother and baby. A baby loves the closeness of taking baths with you in your tub. Draw the warm water to just below your breast level, and allow your baby to float slightly nestled in your arms. Nurse her if she wants. This water ritual is relaxing for both of you, especially during a baby's fussy periods.

I generally discourage using powders and oils on a baby's skin because it is naturally oily and excess oil may attract bacteria. Powders, if inhaled, may be irritating to a baby's sensitive lungs. If you find that your baby's skin is becoming excessively dry, you may be washing her too often and rubbing too hard and thus removing much of the natural oils from her skin. Scented oils and powders may mask the natural baby scent mothers usually find so appealing. Babies love an oil massage *before* the bath. The beautiful ritual of massaging babies is described in Vimala Schneider McClure's *Infant Massage* (see Bibliography).

Care of the Navel

Your baby's cord will fall off sometime between one and three weeks of age. Twice a day, clean around the cord, digging deep into the crevices with a cotton-tipped applicator. Use the antiseptic solution your doctor recommends. It is normal to notice a few drops of blood when the cord falls off, but this will subside within a day or two. After the cord falls off, continue applying the antiseptic solution for a few days until the entire area in the umbilicus is dry.

Circumcision

Up until recent years circumcision was considered a routine procedure for newborn males, but parents are beginning to ask if circumcision is really necessary for their babies. In the following discussion, I will present some information and considerations by which parents can make an informed choice regarding circumcision.

Biblical Basis for Circumcision

Genesis 17:10–12, 14 are the master verses dealing with circumcision in the Old Testament:

This is My covenant which you shall keep, between Me and you and your descendants after you: Every male child among you shall be circumcised; and you shall be circumcised in the flesh of your foreskins, and it shall be a sign of the covenant between Me and you. He who is eight days old among you shall be circumcised, every male child in your generations. . . . And the uncircumcised male child, who is not circumcised in the flesh of his foreskin, that person shall be cut off from his people; he has broken My covenant.

It is clear from this verse that, according to Mosaic law in the Old Testament, God commanded all males to be circumcised.

However, in the New Testament, many verses state that circumcision is not necessary: "Circumcision is nothing and uncircumcision is nothing. . . . Let each one remain in the same calling in which he was called" (1 Cor. 7:19–20); "Circumcision is that of the heart" (Rom. 2:29; see also Gal. 5:6; 6:15). As evidenced in Acts 15, there was much controversy about circumcision among the early Christians. The Pharisees believed that the Mosaic law should be followed and that a Christian could not be saved unless he was circumcised (Acts 15:1, 5). Paul, however, taught that it was not necessary for salvation (1 Cor. 7:18; Gal. 5:2). It seems that the Mosaic law was followed concerning Jesus' circumcision: "On the eighth day, when it was time to circumcise him, he was named Jesus" (Luke 2:21 NIV).

The religious necessity for circumcision was even more controversial in New Testament times than the medical necessity of circumcision is today. There is enough evidence in the New Testament for anyone to conclude that circumcision is not necessary for salvation. Scripture says nothing about circumcision being important for bodily hygiene. Circumcision for the Hebrews was a *blood rite*—a sacrifice symbolic of the blood covenant God made with Abraham. It was never intended to be a health or hygienic measure. For Christians this covenant is made obsolete by the new covenant of Jesus' blood sacrifice on the cross. (For more information on Christianity and circumcision, contact: Peaceful Beginnings, 13020 Homestead Court, Anchorage, Alaska 99516; phone: 907-345-4813.)

Is Circumcision Necessary?

The American Academy of Pediatrics has taken the stand that routine circumcision is an unnecessary procedure. Some parents still ask their pediatricians to help them make a decision regarding circumcision. The following questions and answers are intended to help you make this decision.

1. *How is the circumcision performed?* The baby is placed on a restraining board, and his hands and feet

are secured by straps. The tight adhesions between the foreskin and the penis are separated with a metal instrument. The foreskin is held in place by metal clamps while a cut is made into the foreskin to about one-third of its length. A metal bell is placed over the head of the penis, and the foreskin is pulled up over the bell and cut circumferentially. About one-third of the skin of the penis (called the foreskin) is removed.

2. *Is circumcision safe? Does it hurt?* Circumcision is usually a very safe surgical procedure, and there are rarely any complications. However, as with any surgical procedure, there are occasional problems such as bleeding, infection, or injury to the penis. Yes, it does hurt. If the skin is clamped and cut, of course it hurts. A newborn baby has painful sensations in the skin of his penis, and it is unrealistic to convince yourself that this procedure does not hurt. God has endowed babies with a mechanism by which they can withdraw from pain. Many babies will initially scream and then withdraw into a deep sleep toward the end of the operation.

3. *Can the baby have an anesthesia to lessen the pain?* Yes. A *local anesthesia* can be used. Ask your doctor about this. Although many physicians do not use local anesthesia, painless circumcision should be a birthright. If your doctor is not aware of this technique, he or she can find a description of the procedure in the *Journal of Pediatrics,* vol. 92 (1978), page 998.

4. *Does circumcision make hygiene easier?* The glands in the foreskin secrete a fluid called "smegma." In the adolescent and adult male these secretions may accumulate beneath the foreskin but are easily cleansed during bathing.

What happens if the foreskin is left intact? Leaving the foreskin intact protects the glans from excoriation and infection from diaper rash. At birth it is impossible to make a judgment about how tight the foreskin will remain since almost all boys have tight foreskins for the first few months. But by one year of age in about 50 percent of boys, the foreskin loosens from the head of the penis and retracts completely. By three years of age, 90 percent of uncircumcised boys have fully retractable foreskins. Once the foreskin retracts easily, it becomes a normal part of male hygiene to pull back the foreskin and cleanse beneath it during a bath. While it is true that infection from the secretions beneath the foreskin is more often a problem in uncircumcised males, simple hygiene can prevent this problem.

5. *If the foreskin does not retract naturally, will he need a circumcision later on?* Circumcision is *very rarely* necessary for medical reasons, but when the foreskin does not retract, it becomes tight and infected and obstructs the flow of urine. This condition, called "phimosis," requires circumcision. However, if circumcision for phimosis is necessary later in childhood or adulthood, an anesthesia is given, and the boy is involved in the decision process.

6. *If he isn't circumcised, won't he feel different from his friends?* Parents cannot predict how their son will feel if he is circumcised or intact. Children generally have a wider acceptance of individual differences than adults do. It is difficult to predict whether the majority of boys will be circumcised or intact in the future. The number of circumcised boys has been steadily declining in recent years as more parents begin to question routine circumcision.

7. *My husband is circumcised. Shouldn't my son be the same as his father?* Some fathers have strong feelings that if they are circumcised, their sons should be, and

these feelings should be explored. However, many fathers change their minds once they are fully informed.

8. *We have a son who is already circumcised. Should brothers in the same family be the same?* Many parents feel that sameness is very important among the males of the family since little boys do in fact compare the styles of their penises. Your problem will most likely not be in explaining to your intact child why he is intact but rather in explaining to your circumcised child why he was circumcised.

9. *Do circumcised boys experience any particular problems?* The foreskin acts as a protective covering of the sensitive head of the penis. Removal of the protective foreskin allows the head of the penis to come in contact with ammonia in the diapers. Sometimes this irritation causes circumcised babies to develop painful sores on the tip of the penis that may obstruct the flow of urine.

10. *Does circumcision prevent any disease?* Circumcision does not prevent cancer of the penis. Cancer of the penis is a very rare disease anyway, and it occurs more frequently in males who do not practice proper hygiene. Circumcision does not prevent cervical cancer. Cancer of the cervix is not more common in the sexual partners of intact males who practice proper hygiene. Circumcision also does not prevent venereal disease.

11. *Does circumcision make sex better?* The head of the penis is very sensitive, and this sensitivity may lessen if the protective foreskin has been cut off. Some men who have been circumcised as adults and who compare their sexual experiences before and after have claimed that their penises were more sexually sensitive before the foreskins were removed. Because of this consideration, a custom developed many years ago to do a partial circumcision in which only a small part of the foreskin was removed, thus allowing the foreskin to cover about half of the head of the penis. In my opinion, partial circumcision should not be done because the part of the foreskin still covering the head of the penis may become tighter and the circumcision may have to be repeated later on. This also defeats the purpose of the circumcision because foreskin care is still necessary and adhesions form between the partial foreskin and the head of the penis. In many ritual circumcisions a very generous amount of foreskin is removed. In my experience, more problems arise from circumcisions in which not enough foreskin has been removed than in circumcisions that have removed too much.

12. *When should the circumcision be performed?* Genesis 17:12 states, "He who is eight days old among you shall be circumcised." The probable reason for this was that the newborn baby's blood clots faster by the eighth day. Today, it is medically unnecessary to wait until the eighth day, but for those babies who do not receive an injection of vitamin K shortly after birth, it may be wise to wait until the eighth day for circumcision. Usually circumcision is done in the hospital within the first couple of days after birth at the convenience of all concerned. Up until recent years it was often the custom to do the circumcision immediately after delivery. Because of the increasing regard for the feelings of the newly born baby and the emphasis on the bonding period after birth this practice fortunately is being gradually disregarded. Circumcision shortly after birth is also incompatible with the trend toward gentling the newborn baby and making every attempt to smooth the transition from intrauterine to extrauterine life.

In the previous discussion, I have presented to you my opinion that routine circumcision is neither biblically nor medically indicated. Your individual family custom and desires should be respected. If you are having difficulty deciding whether to circumcise your baby or leave his penis intact, pray to God for wisdom to make this decision. I advise you to consider circumcision with the same prayer and care you would give any other elective surgical procedure for your child.

If you choose to leave your baby's foreskin intact, follow these suggestions on its care. I call this the "uncare" of the foreskin. In most babies the foreskin is tightly adhered to the underlying head of the penis during the first year. The foreskin gradually loosens itself, but it may not fully retract until the second or third year. *Leave the foreskin alone* until it begins to retract easily, which is usually between six months and three years. The age at which the foreskin begins to retract varies considerably from baby to baby. Respect this difference and *do not retract* the foreskin since this may prematurely break the seal between the foreskin and the head of the penis, allowing secretions to accumulate beneath the foreskin. As the foreskin naturally retracts, gently clean out the secretions that may have accumulated between the foreskin and the glans of the penis. This should be done as part of the child's normal bath routine. Usually by three years of age, when most foreskins are fully retracted, a child can easily be taught to clean beneath his foreskin as part of his normal bath routine.

If you choose circumcision, pay close attention to the instructions given to you on how to care for the circumcision site until it is completely healed, usually about one week. The hospital staff will likely give you a starter supply of sterilized gauze pads coated with petroleum jelly that you will wrap around the tip of the penis and change when you change your baby's diaper. If you notice any unusual discharge or foul odor, contact your child's pediatrician.

Part 3

Feeding
Your
Newborn

CHAPTER 10

FEEDING YOUR INFANT

In her baby's first year, the mother will spend more time feeding her infant than she will doing any other parenting task. Feeding your baby according to God's design helps you enjoy this relationship more. This chapter deals with what type of milk to feed your baby. When to administer solid food, and what kinds of foods to avoid.

Mother's Milk

Let me make a very important point at the outset. In my opinion, unless a medical problem prevents it, every baby should be fed his mother's milk as often and as long as the baby wishes and the mother is able. Parents have heard confusing advice about what milk to feed their babies. They have been told that mother's milk is best but that scientifically produced milk is as good. This just isn't true. I sincerely feel that one of the most important gifts you can give your baby is your breast milk. The following pages will present my defense for feeding human milk to human babies.

Breast Milk Is God's Design for Each Species

God designed a total nutrient that is unique to each species. It is the oldest living recipe formulated especially for survival. This nutrient is called "milk." Just as the human mother has the complete capability of nourishing her baby for nine months *in utero,* she also is capable of completely nourishing her infant for at least nine months after birth. Each species has the capacity to feed its young until they triple their birth weight, which humans reach by the age of nine to twelve months.

The milk for each species is suitable for its particular environment. Seal milk is high in fat because seals need high body fat to adapt to their cold environment. The milk of cows and of other range mammals is high in minerals and protein because rapid bone and muscle growth is necessary for their mobility and survival—the calf is up and running within hours after birth. And human milk is high in protein, fat, sugar, and minerals to promote growth in the brain, the survival organ of our species. Only recently have scientists recognized this singular function of human milk, and I feel it is the tip of the iceberg of information left to discover.

Breast Milk Is a Dynamic, Changing, Living Tissue

Breast milk changes as your infant changes. Formula is static; it does not change. An example of this dynamic process is the change in your milk's fat content. Fat accounts for a large percentage of your milk's calories. The hungrier your baby is, the higher the fat content of your milk is. If your baby is only thirsty, he will suckle in such a way that he receives the thinner "skim milk." Your milk has a higher fat content in the morning, and your baby is usually hungrier in the morning. Your milk gradually becomes lower in fat as your baby gets older because he will need fewer calories per pound of body weight as he grows.

Your milk also changes to protect your baby against germs. He needs a supply of germ-fighting elements in his blood called "immunoglobulins." The immuno-globulins, which are unique to each species, protect your baby from the germs in his environment to which he is most susceptible. Shortly after birth your infant begins making his own immunoglobulins, but they do not reach sufficient levels to protect him until he is about six months old. To make up for this deficiency, God has designed the mother to give her baby her immunoglobulins until he is able to make his own, through her blood while he is in the womb and through her milk after he is born.

The very first milk your baby receives shortly after birth is called "colostrum," which is very high in immu-noglobulins. Since your newborn baby is particularly vulnerable to germs, God has designed your milk to be most protective when your baby needs it most. Your colostrum may be considered your baby's first immuni-zation.

Long ago, mother's milk also was known as "white blood," because it contains the same living white cells that blood contains. The white blood cells in your milk keep germs from entering your baby's intestines and fight germs that enter the blood. The white cells also produce a special protein called "immunoglobulin A," which coats your baby's intestines, preventing the pas-sage of harmful germs from his intestines into his blood.

The Chemistry of Breast Milk

Certain chemical nutrients are found in all milk: fat, protein, carbohydrates, minerals, iron, and vitamins. The relative percentages of these nutrients vary in each species' milk according to that species' individual needs.

1. *Fats.* You have read previously how the fat content of your milk changes to meet your baby's changing requirements. Your milk also contains enzymes that help the fat to be digested completely. Because formula does not contain these enzymes, the fat in formula or cow's milk is not totally digested and some passes into the stools, accounting for the unpleasant odor of the stools of formula-fed infants. The lower fat content and the difference in sugars and bacteria in the stools of a breastfed baby account for the sweeter smell. When I smell the stool of a formula-fed infant, I think that the lower end of the intestines has simply rejected part of what went in at the upper end, and the parents' negative reaction to messy diaper changes certainly will not go unnoticed by the egocentric infant.

The cholesterol issue is an example of how scientists have become confused in their efforts to "humanize" the milk that the Creator designed for cows. We know that adults who have high cholesterol in their blood and diets are more prone to heart and blood vessel diseases; therefore, scientists decided to make baby formulas low in cholesterol on the theory that it would prevent heart disease. However, breast milk is much higher in cholesterol than cow's milk or scientifically produced formulas. Common sense dictates that the milk designed and adapted for the survival of a species would not contain a nutrient that could harm it.

Scientists have studied what happens when some newborn rats are fed diets low in cholesterol and some are fed diets high in cholesterol. The results showed that God was right after all: the newborn rats fed high-cholesterol diets actually had lower amounts of cholesterol in their blood when they reached adulthood; whereas, the newborn rats fed low-cholesterol diets actually had higher blood cholesterol as older rats. Formula manufacturers are still uncertain what to make of these studies.

2. *Protein.* Since cows grow four times faster than humans, the amount of the protein casein in cow's milk is four times that of human milk. The curd produced from a mother's milk is smaller and more digestible than that of cow's milk or formula, which is why mothers have observed that the formula-fed baby remains "full" longer than the breastfed baby. Researchers are also just beginning to isolate the amino acid taurine in human milk, which stimulates brain growth.

3. *Carbohydrates.* The predominant sugar in breast milk is lactose. Researchers have noted that mammals with larger brains have a larger percentage of lactose in their milk. Human milk contains more lactose than cow's milk; that is why it tastes sweeter. To make the sweetness similar to mother's milk, cane sugar is added to some formulas, but all sugars are not the same. Cane sugar is digested more rapidly than lactose, and it is known that some older children have mood swings when they eat cane sugar. Perhaps the infant also has blood sugar swings from eating cane sugar in formula.

Lactose also favors the development of certain beneficial bacteria in your baby's intestines. This is known as the "ecology of the gut." It is interesting that God has designed certain bacteria that can live in your baby's intestines provided they have the ideal chemical conditions. These bacteria ward off other bacteria that cause diarrhea. The combination of the artificial, acid-forming sugars and the excess fat in the stools of formula-fed babies often accounts for the "acid burn" diaper rash that is common among them. I sincerely feel God did not design babies' bottoms to look as uncomfortable as they often do.

4. *Minerals.* Cow's milk is high in calcium and phosphorous because cows have a much higher rate of bone growth than humans. These excess mineral salts add an extra load to your infant's immature kidneys. Maybe God foresaw that mothers would not stick to the recipe. He designed for their young; therefore, He made kidneys much larger than necessary to rid the body of its excesses. Your milk is lower in mineral salts and therefore is easier on your newborn's kidneys.

5. *Iron.* Your baby needs iron to make new red blood cells as she grows. As your baby was developing *in utero*, she received a lot of iron from your blood through the placenta. She uses up these iron stores within her first six months; therefore, she needs extra iron. The iron in your breast milk is different from any other kind of iron. Babies who are fed breast milk very rarely become anemic; whereas, babies fed cow's milk or formula without iron often will become anemic between one and two years of age.

The same amount of iron in formula and in breast milk has entirely different effects on a baby. Your baby can absorb only 10 percent of the iron in formula or cow's milk compared to 50 percent of the iron in breast milk. The reason for this difference is that God has provided in your milk a special protein called "lactoferin" that attaches to the iron in your milk. It helps your baby's intestines absorb the iron, thus protecting your baby against anemia; whereas, the excess iron in formula is excreted in the stools. This accounts for the green color of a formula-fed baby's stool. A baby's stools neither look right nor smell right when her intestines are called upon to handle milk they were not designed to handle. Excess iron in the intestines allows harmful bacteria (that can cause severe diarrhea) to thrive in your baby's intestines.

6. *Vitamins.* Breast milk contains all the essential vitamins your baby needs so that vitamin supplements are not necessary in breast-fed infants.

The Advantages of Breastfeeding

Breastfeeding helps mothers know their child better. They learn to determine when their child is full by watching for signs of contentment rather than counting ounces of formula. The mother and her nursing baby have a greater potential for being in harmony with each other, and they establish a trust in their mother-baby dialogue.

Mothers, you become a giving person, and you enjoy this giving because you notice the peace and joy breastfeeding gives you and your baby. Isaiah 66:11–13 beautifully illustrates this feeling of rightness:

That you may feed and be satisfied
With the consolation of her bosom,
That you may drink deeply and be delighted
With the abundance of her glory. (v. 11)

Mothers who practice unrestricted breastfeeding have higher prolactin levels in their blood. The discovery that a nursing baby causes a chemical change within the mother is another example of how science is finally catching up with what God designed and with what intuitive mothers have known all along: something good happens to mothers and babies when they spend more time together.

Mothers often will describe breastfeeding as a loving event with their babies. Here is how my wife, Martha, describes this very special relationship.

God's design for breastfeeding goes beyond physical and emotional benefits. It is His way of bringing each new child into a love relationship with Himself.

We have been teaching our baby to love. When she hears the word, she responds by placing her head against the person holding her. To her, *love* means warmth, holding, closeness, gentleness, and a crooning "ah-h-h." This didn't just happen overnight. She has been learning this little by little since day one.

Psalm 22:9 says, "But You are He who took Me out of the womb; / You made Me trust while on My mother's breasts." Breastfeeding continues the nurturing begun by God in the womb, and it begins the trust relationship that is so vital for the love relationship to develop. A breastfeeding mother is giving herself totally, and the baby gets the message. That message eventually will translate into the concept of love from God: the mother teaches the baby first to trust, then to be loved, then to show love to others, and finally to understand what it means to love God our Father and to be loved by Him. Our baby won't understand all of this for a long time, but even at age sixteen months when she looks at a picture of Jesus and we say, "Jesus loves you," she smiles. When we say, "Erin loves Jesus," she puts her head down on the book and snuggles. To this growing child, the concept of love will not be abstract, and the concept of love from and for God will be real. It all begins with the kind of love God teaches us about in the Bible. First Corinthians 13:4–7 says,

> *Love suffers long and is kind; love does not envy; love does not parade itself, is not puffed up; does not behave rudely, does not seek its own, is not provoked, thinks no evil; does not rejoice in iniquity, but rejoices in the truth; bears all things, believes all things, hopes all things, endures all things.*

John 3:16 says that "God so loved the world that He gave His only begotten Son"—He *gave* Himself. And John 15:13 says, "Greater love has no one than this, than to lay down one's life for his friends." A daily willingness to lay down your life for your baby means *giving of yourself.* John 15:12 says, "This is My commandment, that you love one another as I have loved you."

God designed us to do this as mothers. He gave us breasts to enable us to nourish our babies with *ourselves.* The breasts that our babies suckle are our own flesh. As we give ourselves, our Creator reinforces that love is basic and vital to our babies.

Tips for Successful Breastfeeding

Why are some breastfeeding relationships more successful than others? Throughout the past ten years

I have kept records of the most successful breastfeeding relationships in my practice and the reasons for their success. The following features were common among them.

1. Involvement in natural childbirth classes and La Leche League meetings
2. A positive birthing experience
3. Rooming-in and demand-feeding after birth
4. Correct latch-on, proper positioning, and sucking techniques soon after birth
5. No supplemental bottles unless medically necessary
6. Unscheduled demand-feedings
7. Sleep-sharing
8. A supportive husband
9. A strong mother-infant attachment
10. Prayer and consultation during the breastfeeding relationship

Preparation and Education

The most supportive and knowledgeable mothers' group about breastfeeding is the La Leche League International (see p. 26). Mothers are strongly advised to attend their series of meetings midway through pregnancy and to purchase their book, *The Womanly Art of Breastfeeding*. The mother may wish to continue attending the monthly league meetings for continued advice and support after her infant's birth. In my opinion, this is the best support group for all-around sound mothering advice.

Be confident. Breastfeeding is a natural biological relationship that God has designed for the mother to nourish her baby. Breastfeeding often is described as a confidence game, and prayer is the best confidence-builder.

Getting the Right Start

The following suggestions will help you as a new mother learn how to breastfeed your baby most comfortably.

1. *Begin early.* Unless a medical complication prevents it, begin breastfeeding immediately after birth.

2. *Forget the clock.* Only your baby will know how long and how often he or she should nurse. Ignore the commonly given advice of "begin one minute and gradually increase the time each day so you won't get sore." In the first few days, every baby has a different suck. Some begin sucking enthusiastically immediately after birth; others snooze and lick for the first day. It is not how *long* a baby sucks but *how* he sucks that can cause sore nipples.

3. *Position yourself.* If you are able, sitting up in bed is your easiest position for nursing. Pillows are a real must. Place them behind your back, head, and on your lap for your baby, and under the arm that will support your baby. Get comfortable before beginning to nurse. You may be more comfortable lying on your side, especially if you have had a cesarean section. Several breastfeeding pillows are now commercially available. These pillows are designed to wrap around the mother's midsection and for the baby to lie on top of the pillow, perfectly positioned to reach the breast. While standard pillows can serve the same purpose, many women appreciate the convenience of these specially designed products.

4. *Position your baby.* Undress your baby to promote skin-to-skin contact. Nestle him in your arm so that his head rests in the bend of your elbow, his back along your forearm, and his buttocks in your hand. His head should be straight, not arched backward or turned in relation to the rest of his body. Your baby should not have to turn his head and strain to reach your nipple (turn your head to the side or up toward the ceiling and try to swallow!). Turn his entire body so he is facing you tummy to tummy. His head and body should face your breast directly, as if an imaginary line were drawn from the center of your breast to the center of your nipple to the center of his mouth. To further this close contact, tuck your baby's lower arm alongside his body in the soft pocket of your midriff so that it is out of the way.

5. *Support your breast.* Cup your breast with the other hand, supporting your breast from underneath with only your thumb on top. Be sure your hand stays way back, clear of the areola. It is important to continue holding your breast throughout the feeding until your baby is old enough and strong enough to manage the weight of your breast himself. Manually express a few drops of milk to moisten the nipple.

6. *Use the correct latch-on.* Incorrect latch-on is the most frequent cause of an unrewarding breastfeeding relationship. Using your nipple as a teaser, gently tickle your baby's lips with your milk-moistened nipple, encouraging him to open his mouth widely (babies' mouths often open like little birds' beaks—very wide—and then quickly close). The moment your baby opens his mouth widely, direct your nipple into his mouth (be sure to place it above his tongue), and *quickly draw him very close* to you with the arm that is holding him (see figures). If you don't do it quickly enough the little mouth will close and you'll have to start over. Don't

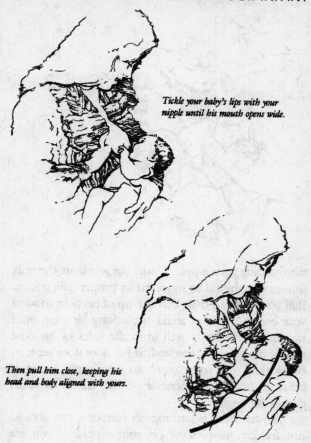

Tickle your baby's lips with your nipple until his mouth opens wide.

Then pull him close, keeping his head and body aligned with yours.

lean forward, pushing your breast toward your baby. Pull him toward you. Most new mothers do not pull their babies close enough.

Attempt to get a large part of your areola into his mouth. The key to correct latch-on is for your baby to suck on the areola, the dark area of your breast

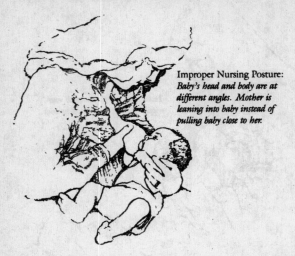

Improper Nursing Posture: *Baby's head and body are at different angles. Mother is leaning into baby instead of pulling baby close to her.*

surrounding your nipple. Under the areola are the milk sinuses that should be squeezed for proper milk release. Pull your baby so close that the tip of his nose touches your breast. Don't be afraid of blocking his nose, since he can breathe quite well from the sides of his nose even if the tip is compressed. If his nose does seem to be blocked, use your thumb to press gently on your breast to uncover his nose or pull his feet in closer to change his angle.

If your baby is latching on correctly, you should not feel painful pressure on your nipple. If you are feeling that the baby is sucking mostly on your nipple, push down on his lower jaw and lip to open his mouth wider. You should notice an instant relief from the pain. If your baby does not cooperate, break the suction and start again. Some babies do not detach themselves readily. You need to break the seal by sliding your finger into the corner of baby's mouth and between his gums.

If you just pull baby off you may damage your nipple. Because improper latch-on will cause sore nipples, it is important that he learn the right way. Most babies learn to suck as a natural instinct, but some babies have to be taught to latch on properly. If you have sore nipples that are getting worse, seek help from a La Leche League leader or a lactation consultant.

Sucking Styles

After a few weeks you will notice that your baby exhibits two kinds of sucking: comfort sucking, a weaker suck primarily with the lips in which your baby gets the foremilk; and the nutritive sucking, a more vigorous sucking with the whole jaw. You will notice the muscles of his face working so hard that even his ears wiggle during intense nutritive sucking. This kind of more productive sucking rewards the baby with the higher-calorie hindmilk (the creamy milk that comes later in the feeding after the milk ejection reflex has been activated by the strong nutritive sucking). The visible contractions of your baby's jaw muscles and the audible swallow sounds (little gulping noises from his throat after every one to three sucking efforts) are reliable indications that your baby has good suckling techniques and that he is getting milk.

Alternative Nursing Positions

If you have had a cesarean section, it may be easier for you to nurse your baby lying down. Turn on your side and ask the nurse to position some pillows between your back and the bed rail, another pillow between your knees, and try an extra pillow under your head. Some mothers also want pillows supporting their abdomens. Ask the nurse to place your baby on her side facing you and nestled in your arm, and slide your baby up or down until her mouth lines up with your nipple area. Pick up and support your breast as mentioned previously, then tickle her mouth open with your nipple. When her mouth opens widely, pull your baby toward you, inserting your nipple and areola into her mouth.

Another alternative nursing arrangement for a mother who is unable to stand the pressure of her baby on her incision after a cesarean, or for a baby who has difficulty latching on, is the "football hold" or clutch hold (see figure). While sitting up, place a pillow under your arm and your baby on the pillow. Cup the back of his neck in your hand and let his legs rest against the pillow supporting your back. Follow the same procedure for proper latch-on as mentioned above. This clutch hold works particularly well for babies who squirm, arch their backs, and frequently detach themselves from the breast.

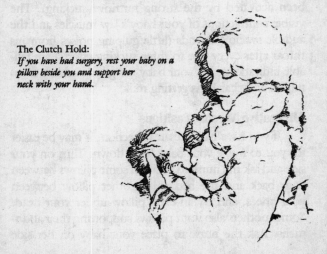

The Clutch Hold:
If you have had surgery, rest your baby on a pillow beside you and support her neck with your hand.

Some babies latch on to the breast and suck properly within the first day or so; other babies are slow starters and suck a little and snooze a little. These babies need to have a little prodding and need skin-to-skin contact in their mothers' arms. With constant encouragement, the sleepy baby gradually will suck longer and more enthusiastically.

How to Care for Your Nipples

Teaching your baby to latch on correctly to your areola and your nipple is the best preventive medicine for sore nipples. If your baby's mouth is open wide enough and if he is drawn close enough to your breast, his jaws will be compressing the areola rather than your nipple. There is no need for special cleansing of your breast either before or after nursing. The little bumps on your areola around your nipple are glands that secrete a cleansing and lubricating oil to protect the nipples and keep them clean. Daily bathing or showering is all that is necessary to keep your breasts and nipples clean. Avoid using soap on your nipples since it may encourage dryness and cracking. After nursing, let your nipples dry thoroughly before you put your bra flap up. You may find nursing pads helpful to continue to wick away leakage and keep nipples dry between feedings.

The best massage mediums for sore or sensitive nipples are your own breast milk or a drop or two of vitamin E oil from a capsule massaged completely into the skin two to three times a day after feeding. It is not necessary to wash this oil off before the next nursing. Massaging stimulates circulation, which encourages healing. Be sure the cup of your nursing bra is not too small or too tight. Tight clothing will compress your

133

breasts and encourage plugged ducts and infection. Cotton bras allow air to reach the sore nipples, and you may need to use a breast cup or shell to keep the nipple free of any clothing. Call La Leche League for help.

Formula-Feeding

Although I believe that breastfeeding with infant-led weaning is God's design for infant nutrition, the commercially prepared infant formulas are relatively safe and effective as an alternative source of nutrition for most infants. But because formula is a static nutrient and breast milk is a dynamically changing nutrient, formula is *only a distant second best*. Formulas are prepared using cow's milk or certain legumes, such as soybeans, as a protein base. Vitamins, minerals, and chemically processed portions of various nutrients are added to "humanize" the infant formula.

Commercial formulas are available in three forms: powdered formula with directions on adding water, concentrated liquid formula that should be mixed half and half with water, and ready-to-feed formulas that can be poured directly into a bottle. Your doctor will help you choose which formula is best for your baby. A word of caution: *never mix the formula in greater strength than the directions advise*. Always add the specified amount of water. Adding too little water makes the formula too concentrated for your baby's immature kidneys and intestines to handle and may make him sick. Babies usually like their formula slightly warmed, like breast milk. Iron-fortified formulas should be used unless your doctor advises otherwise.

"How Much Formula Should I Feed My Baby?"

The amount of formula your infant will drink will depend upon his weight and his appetite. Use the following rule of thumb for your baby's first six months: *two to two and a half ounces of formula per pound per day.* For example, if your baby weighs ten pounds, he may take twenty to twenty-five ounces of formula per day. This amount may change from day to day. After six months, the daily volume of formula probably will remain the same or gradually diminish as your baby's volume of solid food increases.

Demand-feeding also applies to formula-fed babies. In demand-feeding an infant is fed every time her or his little tummy desires. In scheduled feeding, a baby is fed every three to four hours at preassigned times according to mother's convenience and baby's appetite. A third alternative is the semi-demand schedule in which your baby has one or two preassigned feedings and is fed on demand between them.

Formula-fed babies can be put on a schedule more easily since formula is digested more slowly. Demand-feeding caters to your infant's satisfaction; scheduled feeding is for your convenience and your own individual family situation. Most formula-feeding mothers elect the compromise of a semi-demand type of schedule. During the first few weeks they wake their babies for feedings during the day, if they sleep more than four to five hours, to discourage the exhausting feeding pattern of a day sleeper and night feeder. Frequent feedings during the day and bottles at 7:00 P.M. and at 11:00 P.M. seem to be the most comfortable feeding schedule for most parents.

135

Feeding time should be a time of special closeness. As in breastfeeding, talk to your baby; look at him and caress him during your bottle-feeding. You may partially undress yourself and your baby and hold him in close, skin-to-skin contact on your breast even though you are bottle-feeding. Remember, not only the kind of milk your infant gets is important but also how he gets it. Above all, resist the temptation to prop the bottle for your baby to drink alone. Not only is this practice unsafe, it is not nurturing.

"What About Vitamin and Fluoride Supplements?"

Commercial infant formulas contain all the vitamins necessary for your infant, but remember that in order for your baby to receive the daily recommended amount of vitamins, she has to take the entire can of formula. Many babies do not consume an entire can of formula every day until they are a few months old; so, vitamin supplements may be recommended by their pediatricians. In later infancy and childhood many children have erratic diets, eating well one day and poorly the next. Your pediatrician will recommend vitamins according to your child's individual needs. Fluoride supplements may or may not be prescribed by your physician depending upon how much fluoride is in your drinking water and upon how much water your child drinks.

Breastfed babies do not need vitamin supplements. If your nutrition is adequate, your milk contains all the necessary vitamins and nutrients your infant will need for her first six to nine months.

Iron is necessary to make new red blood cells and to replenish the used-up iron that came from your blood *in utero*. Formula-fed infants should receive iron-fortified formulas from birth on, or at least from four months on. Parents may feel occasionally that the added iron causes gastrointestinal upsets in their infants, although controlled studies comparing iron-fortified formulas and formulas without iron showed no difference in the number of intestinal problems. If the iron-fortified formula does not agree with your baby, iron-rich foods, such as meat and iron-fortified cereal, may be offered to your baby at the age of five or six months, according to your pediatrician's suggestion. Iron-fortified formula often gives a baby's stools a green color, but this has no significance. Breastfed infants rarely need iron supplements, at least not during their first six to twelve months.

Now that you have a general understanding of both breastfeeding and formula-feeding, in the next chapter I will move on to answer some questions specific to creating a fulfilling and long-term breastfeeding relationship.

CHAPTER 11

COMMON BREASTFEEDING QUESTIONS AND SPECIAL CIRCUMSTANCES

■ Although breastfeeding was designed by God to be the perfect feeding method for your child, it does take some practice and is not always the most natural or comfortable thing to do. Breastfeeding *should* be completely comfortable and natural but you may need some sound advice and persistence to make it so. In this chapter I will answer some of the common questions I hear in my practice about breastfeeding and offer some solutions to some specific nursing nuisances.

"When Will My Milk Come In?"

The milk mothers produce immediately after birth is colostrum. Your true milk will appear gradually or quickly some time between the second and the fifth days after your baby's birth, depending on whether this is your first baby, the fatigue level of your birthing experience, how well your baby learns to latch on to your breast, and how frequently and how effectively your baby sucks.

"How Do My Breasts Make Milk?"

Your milk is produced in tiny milk glands throughout your breast. The milk drains into tiny channels that merge into reservoirs beneath your areola called "milk sinuses." Milk empties from these sinuses through approximately twenty openings in your nipple. When your baby sucks, the nerve endings in your nipple stimulate the pituitary gland in your brain, which secretes prolactin. The prolactin stimulates your milk glands to produce more milk. The first milk your baby receives at each feeding is foremilk, which is thin because of its low fat content.

As your baby continues sucking, the nerve endings stimulate the pituitary gland to secrete another hormone called "oxytocin." This hormone causes the tissue around your milk glands to contract like a rubber band and squeeze a larger supply of milk from the milk glands into the sinuses. This latter milk, or hindmilk, is much higher in fat and slightly higher in protein and, therefore, has greater nutritional value. The hindmilk is the primary nutrient for your infant's growth. Most mothers have a tingling sensation in their breasts as the hindmilk is released from the milk glands into the milk sinuses. This is called the "let-down reflex" or "milk-ejection reflex." A successful milk-ejection reflex is key to successful breastfeeding.

"What Happens If I Have Too Much Milk?"

When your milk first appears, your breasts may feel very full because of the presence of milk and because of the swelling of your breast glands. This feeling is called "engorgement." Engorgement is your body's signal to get the milk out. Do not let this engorgement become increasingly painful because continued engorgement can lead to a breast infection. Standing in a hot shower, placing hot towels on your breasts, and encouraging your baby to suck frequently and effectively are the best ways to prevent continued engorgement.

If a breast infection (mastitis) occurs, above all, *don't stop nursing!* Your best prevention and treatment of breast infection is emptying your breasts. Immersing your engorged breasts in comfortably hot water for ten minutes can facilitate emptying. Use cold compresses to alleviate your pain. Use hot compresses and express your milk manually to soften your areola so baby can latch on more easily. If your breasts are rock hard, so that you can't get the milk to flow, you will need to use continuous ice packs until the swelling has subsided enough to allow the milk to get out. If high fever, chills, fatigue, and increasing soreness and redness of your breasts occur, then you may need antibiotics. Call your doctor if you have these symptoms. Your baby still can breastfeed while you are taking antibiotics. Engorgement in the later weeks is often due to an upset in the baby's or the family's routine—too many visitors, missed feedings, excessive use of supplemental formulas—that throws the "timer" out of balance. Continued mother-infant attachment and demand-feeding in which you keep the harmony in tune are the best ways to prevent this uncomfortable engorgement.

"Should My Baby Be on a Feeding Schedule?"

Early in your breastfeeding relationship you will realize that the term *schedule* has absolutely no meaning in breastfeeding a baby. The only schedule your baby will have, and should have, is his own. Remember, breastfeeding is more than a mathematical exercise. One nursing mother put it this way, "I don't count the number of feedings any more than I count the number of kisses."

One of the most beautiful and natural biological negotiations is a mother and a suckling baby working together to get their own biological clocks synchronized and the law of supply and demand working comfortably. Listen to your baby's cues and don't clock-watch.

Breastfeeding cannot be scheduled easily because babies digest breast milk more rapidly than formula; therefore, breastfed babies feel hungry more often and need to be fed more often. Also, babies have growth spurts during which they need more food for more growth. Babies enjoy periods of nonnutritive sucking in which they are more interested in the feel they get than in the food they get. Sometimes babies are only thirsty and suck a little to obtain some of the watery foremilk. Most babies breastfeed every two to three hours around the clock for the first few months. This is one of the many realistic expectations you should have about parenting.

■ What About Parent-Controlled Feedings?

A style of feeding that has recently become popular in some Christian writings is a way of scheduling feedings called "parent-controlled feedings" (PCF).

Nearly every major parenting organization, especially lactation consultants, infant nutritionists, and professionals who counsel breastfeeding mothers, has issued warnings to parents to be aware of the dangers of this type of feeding. Yet, new parents who are vulnerable to the advice of authority figures and eager to do what they believe is best for their baby often fall prey to this misguided nutritional advice. Parent-controlled feedings is scheduling the breastfed baby's feedings similar to those of a bottle-fed baby. This style of feeding is based on the erroneous assumption that there is little difference between breast- and formula-feeding. Because breast milk is digested faster, breastfed babies do need to be fed more often than do formula-fed infants. Also, proponents of this way of feeding use PCF as a discipline tool rather than a nutritional one. It assumes that babies manipulate their parents by their cues to be fed.

This method of feeding ignores two basic biological facts: babies have growth spurts and need more frequent feedings during these spurts and that breast milk is not the same at each feeding. Depending on how hungry the baby is, he or she may nurse longer and more frequently at different times of the day. Finally, PCF ignores time-tested advice. The La Leche League International, the largest and most respected worldwide organization on breastfeeding, has for years denounced this method of feeding for two reasons: babies often do not thrive on rigidly controlled schedules and the mother becomes desensitized to the cues of her baby.

As we have previously said, breastfeeding is an exercise in babyreading. It is not just a delivery of nutrition, it is a way of getting to know your baby. Common sense should tell us that the one who is hungry, baby, should know how often and how long he or she should nurse. Every mother and infant must work out a cue-response system of breastfeeding that works for them. Before blindly following any method of feeding, be sure to first check it out with your healthcare provider. ■

"What If I Don't Have Enough Milk—or Any Milk?"

Most delays in milk production are the result of an interference in the mother's and baby's timers. Giving supplemental bottles, not rooming in, and scheduled feedings are the common causes of delayed lactation. As I am making my hospital rounds and a new mother tearfully expresses that her milk has not come in, I usually approach the well-meaning nurses and ask, "Okay, confess. Who has been slipping this baby a bottle?"

Many times, nurses who do not wish to hear a baby cry will feed the baby a supplemental formula in the nursery. The formula temporarily satisfies the baby's hunger so that by the time he comes to his mother he is not hungry enough and does not suck enthusiastically. As a result the mother's milk production is not stimulated. If your milk is not appearing, keep your baby close to you for as many hours of the day as possible. Take your baby to bed with you and nurse lying down, having skin-to-skin contact with each other. Look at, caress, massage, and groom your baby while you are nursing to stimulate the milk-producing hormones.

Insufficient milk production during the first month may also mean that you are taking on too many outside responsibilities. Reorganize your commitments and priorities and get back into full-time mothering. Pray daily, asking God to give you the commitment and the milk sufficient to mother your baby in the way He has designed. Also, rid your house of negative advisers who drop defeating hints such as, "I couldn't breastfeed my baby either"; "She seems hungry all the time"; "Are you sure she's getting enough milk?" You don't need discouragement when you are trying to build up your confidence as a new mother. Surround yourself with supportive people and go to a La Leche League meeting.

"How Long Should My Baby Nurse?"

The duration of nursing varies from baby to baby because babies' sucking techniques and nutritional requirements vary. Your baby probably will nurse about ten minutes on one breast and five minutes or longer on the other breast. If your baby is an enthusiastic nurser, she will get most of her milk in the first three minutes of nursing. During that time you will have experienced a milk-ejection reflex. The remainder of the time is important for meeting her sucking needs. Less enthusiastic babies require a longer time to get sufficient milk. Also, you may experience a series of small milk-ejection reflexes throughout the feeding rather than one large one. Some babies, especially sleepy babies and small or premature babies, do better with the technique of switch nursing. (See "Why Isn't My Baby Gaining Weight?" page 148.)

"Does My Baby Need an Extra Bottle?"

The breastfed baby usually needs neither a supplemental bottle of formula nor a bottle of water. Formula-fed babies need extra water to wash out all the formula's extra salts that they do not need.

"Why Does My Baby Want to Nurse All the Time?"

In their first few months babies have "frequency days" when all they want to do is nurse. I call this "marathon nursing." This supply-and-demand principle of breastfeeding is working in response to their sudden growth spurts. Some babies may also be going through periods of high-need levels. However, you may soon become exhausted as you try to fulfill your persistently hungry baby's needs. Try the following survival tips.

Be sure your baby is getting mostly milk at each feeding and not a lot of air. Attempt to get more of your hindmilk into your baby to satisfy him longer. (See "Why Isn't My Baby Gaining Weight?" page 148.)

Avoid the "filler food" fallacy. You may be advised to give your baby cereal before bedtime or between nursings or have someone give him a bottle while you catch up on sleep. This is not good advice for your two- or three-month-old baby, and it seldom works anyway. Usually your baby wants and needs more milk, not filler food. Supplemental bottles, if used too frequently, may actually diminish your milk supply and lead to premature weaning. A suddenly increased demand to nurse is often misinterpreted as a need for solid foods, which is not likely to be the case until your baby is four to six months old. Your baby is simply signaling that he needs more milk to meet his sudden growth spurt. By accommodating your baby's demand for more frequent breastfeeding, your supply will increase to meet his demand after a few days; and your supply-and-demand relationship will be reestablished at a higher level of milk production.

Catnap when your baby sleeps. This requires delaying or delegating many of the seemingly pressing household chores. If you are blessed with a baby who nurses frequently, you may think, *I don't get anything done.* But you are getting something done. You are doing the most important job in the world—mothering a human being.

If your baby is a lazy nurser, try the following ideas. (1) Take your baby to bed with you and allow her to nurse a little and sleep a little; (2) undress your baby to promote skin-to-skin contact; (3) sit up in bed at a forty-five-degree angle and nurse if your baby is one of those exhausting babies who awaken as soon as they are put down. You both may sleep in this semi-upright position; or (4) try the burp-and-switch technique, which tends to keep sleepy babies awake long enough to nurse.

"How Do I Know My Baby Is Getting Enough Milk?"

After the first month or two you will know intuitively that your baby is getting enough milk. He will feel and look heavier. In the first few weeks it is not as easy to tell if your baby is getting enough milk, especially if you are a first-time mother. Here are some signs that your baby is getting enough milk in the first few weeks. (1) Your baby will have wet diapers often—at least six or eight wet cloth diapers (four to five wet disposables) and two or more bowel movements per day; (2) your breasts may feel full before feedings, less full after feedings, and leak between feedings; (3) if you feel your baby sucking vigorously, hear him swallowing, feel your milk-ejection reflex, and then see your baby drift contentedly into never-never land, chances are he has gotten enough milk.

"Why Isn't My Baby Gaining Weight?"

The medical term for poor weight gain is *failure to thrive*. This section is about only the breastfed baby who does not have any underlying illness that may cause him or her not to grow. In the first few weeks, most breastfed babies who are not gaining weight properly are getting enough milk but not enough calories. Their mothers worry because their babies nurse regularly but look undernourished. This may be because they are getting only the low-calorie foremilk but not the high-calorie, creamy hindmilk they need to put on weight. These babies are active and require at least six to eight fresh diapers a day; however, they do not have enough body fat, which makes their skin appear to fit loosely over their scrawny-looking muscles. This condition is usually caused by one of two problems: faulty sucking techniques or an inadequate milk-ejection reflex.

Usually, if a breastfed baby fails to thrive, the basic principles for breastfeeding were not carried out successfully. The following suggestions are aimed at increasing the fat content of your milk and improving the efficiency of your baby's sucking.

1. *Improve your diet.*
2. *Get some rest.* This may require reorganizing the household chores and responsibilities that compete with your nursing relationship.

3. *Spend a lot of time in touch with your baby:* skin-to-skin contact, eye-to-eye contact, grooming, caressing, and sleeping together. The more you are together, the more likely your baby is to suckle, which stimulates your prolactin.

4. *Increase the frequency of feedings* to at least one feeding every two to three hours, and wake your baby during the day if she sleeps longer than three hours. Take your baby to bed with you and nurse during the night. Your sleeping baby often will nurse very well when nestled in bed with you away from the competition of a busy world.

5. *Try switch nursing.* In the traditional method of nursing, you encourage your baby to nurse as long as he wishes on one breast (usually about ten minutes) and to complete his feeding on the second breast, reversing the process on the next feeding. Switch nursing, also called the "burp-and-switch technique," operates as follows. Let your baby nurse on the first breast until the intensity of his suck and his swallow diminish and his eyes start to close. Remove him from this breast and burp him well; then, switch to the next breast until his sucking diminishes again and burp him a second time. Repeat the entire process. This burp-and-switch technique encourages a creamier, high-calorie hindmilk to come into your breast at each feeding. The technique is particularly effective for the sleepy baby, or what I call the "slurper-snoozer" or the "poopy sucker." Several times during nursing the milk-ejection reflex brings hindmilk into the second breast so that by the time the baby nurses on the second breast he is rewarded with high-calorie milk. This observation perhaps accounts for the old saying, "Babies grow best on the second breast."

6. *Try techniques of double nursing,* which operate on the same principle of increasing the volume and fat content of the milk. After you nurse your baby and she seems to be content, carry her around in the upright position instead of immediately putting her down to sleep. Burp her well, and about ten minutes later, breastfeed her a second time, putting her down to rest with a fuller tummy. Your baby may regurgitate this larger volume of milk if put down immediately after feeding. In this case either put her in an infant seat, if she will be content, or carry her in a sling-type carrier for twenty to thirty minutes after feeding to allow her stomach to empty.

7. *Correct inefficient sucking techniques.* Most infants instinctively know how to suck properly, but some infants have to be trained. Two bad habits that newborn nursers tend to develop are flutter sucking, which is sucking in short spurts with little or no cheek and jaw action, and nipple chewing.

Efficient sucking requires a baby to draw the areola well into his mouth and compress the milk sinuses under the areola with his lips and jaws. His tongue should compress the milk sinuses against the roof of his mouth and effectively "milk" the milk out of the sinuses, into the nipple, and into his mouth. Some babies do not get enough of the milk sinuses into their mouths or do not effectively compress the sinuses or do not coordinate their tongue actions and swallowing actions. As a result these babies get only the foremilk and do not empty the breasts well at each feeding, and consequently do not grow well. Review the positioning techniques for proper sucking as described in Chapter 10. Also be sure that your breasts are not too full. An engorged breast is difficult to nurse from since your baby is only able to suck on a nub of your nipple and not on soft and compressible areola. If your breasts are too full, manually express some breast milk prior to each feeding in order to soften your areola; also use the milk-moistened nipple as a teaser.

8. *Avoid supplemental formulas* if your baby is not gaining weight properly, unless your doctor advises you otherwise. Introducing bottles too early (within the first two weeks) may cause nipple confusion, further interferes with your breastfeeding relationship, and may wean your baby before her time. Premature babies and babies who fail to thrive as a consequence of faulty sucking may need supplemental formulas until their own sucking mechanisms mature. If your baby needs a supplemental formula, it is best to feed it to her by way of a supplemental nutrition system (SNS), which is a small container that contains formula and hangs around your neck. A tiny spaghettilike plastic tubing runs from the container onto your nipple. As your baby sucks milk from your breast, he also gets formula from the tubing. Having his mouth full of formula trains your baby to suck more vigorously on your breast thereby encouraging him to get more of your own milk. This system, which can be located through your local La Leche League, can be discontinued gradually as your lactation and your baby's sucking techniques improve.

9. *Try prayer and consultation.* If your baby is not thriving on your milk, ask God to bless this special relationship. In my experience, babies do not fail to thrive on breast milk because their mothers are not producing good milk, but because some breastfeeding technique needs to be corrected. Most major cities have lactation specialists, such as La Leche League, who can give you the proper support and advice you need.

All too often, a mother is advised to put her baby on a bottle because he is not growing on her milk. This advice is popular because it gets everybody off the hook, and no one has to work hard at finding the real reason a baby is not growing. Obtain proper consultation from a lactation specialist before succumbing to this advice.

"We're Adopting a Baby—Can I Breastfeed?"

This may come as a surprise to you, but yes, you can. This is accomplished with the use of an SNS. While your baby is receiving formula from the SNS, he also is sucking from your breast. Over a period of several weeks, you gradually will begin to lactate, and the baby will receive nourishment from you as well as the formula. Although an adopting mother seldom can produce enough milk for total nourishment of her baby, the continued sucking causes an increase in her prolactin levels.

Nursing Nuisances

The Curious Baby

Between four and six months of age, babies become so interested in their surroundings that they suck a little and look a little. This nuisance makes nursing seem to last forever, and constant latching on and pulling off may become unpleasant for your nipples. If this curiosity nuisance develops, use the technique of closet nursing. Take your baby into a quiet, dark, and uninteresting room to nurse him when he is susceptible to too much visual stimulation.

The Nursing Strike

Another nursing nuisance that occurs between six and twelve months of age is the nursing strike; your baby may lose interest in nursing for a few days. This strike can come at any time. Don't immediately interpret this strike as the time for weaning. This lack of interest in breastfeeding can be the result of any number of occurrences. Your baby may have a cold or may be teething; he may be reacting to a change in his routine, his environment, or his milk supply; or he may be reacting to a physical or emotional change in you. During this temporary strike, give your baby extra love and security, pump your breasts frequently to keep your milk flowing, and spend a lot of time physically together.

Relax, quit watching the clock, avoid bottles and pacifiers. I advise you again to take your baby to bed with you and offer your breast to him while lying down. Many babies will go off strike when they nurse in bed, especially if they are very sleepy. It sometimes helps to walk around as you breastfeed. A last resort may be to nurse your baby while he is sleeping. These nursing strikes seldom last for more than a few days, but plan to spend all your time with your baby as you win him back to the happy relationship you had before the strike.

The Sleepy Baby

Breastfeeding the sleepy baby is one of the most frustrating nursing nuisances for new mothers. During their first few weeks, some babies like to suck a little and sleep a little and apparently fall asleep before they get enough milk. This problem is common in small infants and premature babies. One of the baby's last mechanisms to mature is the feeding mechanism, so if she is three weeks premature, she actually may require three weeks before she can suck vigorously like a mature baby.

Try the following suggestions for breastfeeding your sleepy baby.

1. Review the positioning techniques described in Chapter 10. Be sure to tickle the sleepy baby's mouth open wide enough for her to get enough of your areola into her mouth. Sleepy babies are also prone to flutter sucking.

2. Undress your baby and yourself to increase the skin-to-skin contact during nursing.

3. Manually express some of your milk before feeding; this will soften your breast and allow your little snoozer to get more of your areola into her mouth and thus get more milk.

4. During the feeding, as your baby's sucking intensity and swallowing diminish, gently prod her by tickling her cheeks and pulling her lower jaw down to help her keep her mouth open wide.

5. Sleepy babies tire easily at the breast and do not adjust well to the usual technique of feeding ten or fifteen minutes on each breast. Sleepy babies feed better with the burp-and-switch technique of breastfeeding.

6. Pray for perseverance. Sleepy babies are a real nuisance to nurse but the nuisance usually lasts only a week or two. Pray for perseverance in your breastfeeding relationship until your baby's sucking mechanism becomes more mature.

The Biter

When your baby is four to six months old and is feeling pressure in his gums from the early phase of teething, your nipple will become a handy teething object. Toothless gums chomping down on your tender breast can be disturbing enough, but cutting teeth justify a complaint—it hurts! Your surprised reaction to the pain—"OUCH!"—is sometimes enough to startle your baby loose, although he may instead clamp down even harder. Just don't overdo the startle effect or you might cause a nursing strike. You can quickly and smoothly disengage your baby's viselike grip by pushing down on his lower jaw with your thumb. An alternative technique is to pull your baby quickly into your breast very close as soon as you sense he is clamping down. This "reverse psychology" requires him to let go if he wants to breathe. Being removed from your breast and hearing various sounds of disapproval will train your baby out of this pastime. You probably will find that he does this toward the end of a feeding or when he is not really hungry but just fussy from teething discomfort. Substitute a less sensitive object if he is desperate to have his gums eased.

Feeding the High-Need Newborn

Some new babies are a complete shock to their mothers. No mother can be prepared fully for the changes a new baby is going to bring into her life. Only as she experiences life with the new baby does she begin to realize what's in store for her as a first-time mom (or as a practiced mom who is having her first high-need baby). A friend calls to congratulate her on her new blessing and she replies, "You won't believe how much this little one needs. I can't put him down, as soon as I do he's awake and cries as though I've never fed him." This kind of baby needs to be nursed constantly and held constantly. One exhausted mother had a little energy left for humor and told me, "It's one constant holdathon."

After about three days at home with your high-need newborn, you might think, *I need some sleep; I can't keep this up; I'm going crazy; I'm desperate, exhausted, and look like death warmed over.* You may not know if the problem is within you (your breast, your milk, your mind) or within your baby (his sucking technique or his ability to concentrate long enough to suck enough milk). All you will want to do is give your baby a bottle, fill him up one time so he will sleep three hours (you thought all new babies did that) so you can sleep without hearing him cry five minutes after you put him down. One mother shared with me, "I can't even put him down long enough to go to the bathroom." Let's look at your options at this point.

Supplement with a Bottle of Formula

The usual advice is "Just give the baby a full tummy once so you can get caught up on your sleep, recharge your batteries, and carry on." This seems to work, and the baby sleeps for two to three hours at a stretch, or maybe more. The problem with this option is that it is a short-term gain with a risk for a long-term loss. It does nothing to help the next day or the next, and actually it can hurt your milk supply because the supply-and-demand mechanism has been tampered with. All you may find out with this option is what you already knew—formula stays in the baby's tummy longer than breast milk. The fact that your baby slept longer with formula does not mean that you did not have enough breast milk. All it means is that you're not giving her a whole day of leisurely sucking. Your baby needs that sucking more than most babies and that is why she wakes up so quickly when the sucking and the warm arms disappear. Consider a very important fact: you are aiming for a long-term breastfeeding relationship. Getting your baby hooked on too many bottles too soon jeopardizes your entire breastfeeding relationship. In my experience, giving supplemental bottles to babies younger than six weeks of age often leads to premature weaning. Many nursing mothers need six weeks of total breastfeeding before their milk supplies are stable enough to withstand an occasional supplemental bottle.

Stop Breastfeeding?

You can stop breastfeeding, which is probably what will happen anyway if you keep giving the baby a bottle just to fill him up. He soon will prefer sucking from a rubber nipple and will want to suck less and less on your nipple. As a result, you sacrifice the supply-and-demand relationship that is working for you, at least on a marginal basis.

Do you really *want* to breastfeed? Remember, breastfeeding is 95 percent attitude. Why do you want to breastfeed? Is it because all your friends are breastfeeding and will think you are a bad mother or a failure as a woman if you don't? Or because your husband thinks it is the only way your baby is going to be raised? If your answer is honestly one of these reasons, you won't be happy breastfeeding and neither will your baby. You must be happy for him to be happy, especially since you are getting such a shaky start, which may in fact be due to your own inner unwillingness to breastfeed. You have to *want* to breastfeed, first for your baby's best, and second for your own self-fulfillment.

If you decide to bottle-feed your baby, you should be supported in your decision. But realize that switching to the bottle does not guarantee that your high-need baby will automatically become easier to handle. He may sleep more regularly for a day or two or a week or two; but if his basic temperament is that of a high-need baby, he still will be temperamental, and you may wonder if your baby would have benefited from all the early holding and nursing you could have given him had you stuck it out.

Stick with Breastfeeding!

This may not be the option your body or mind (what is left of it) wants to consider, but in your spirit you may say, "Yes, I want to stick with breastfeeding." You may have to spend some time in prayer and counsel before wholeheartedly reaching this decision because it is a choice that definitely affects your spirit. You'll need help and lots of it; first, from your heavenly Father and, second, from someone who has overcome the same obstacles you are facing. Call the La Leche League and ask to be put in touch with a leader in your area who has nursed a baby like yours. She will tell you what helped her, and if she did it, you can do it. Remember, nursing is something you can do if you want to do it for the right reasons. If you don't, it is not worth the physical, emotional, and spiritual energy you'll have to invest and that you simply may not have.

So you choose to stick it out and you are back to

square one. You can't put your baby down because he wakes and cries five minutes after you do, but you can't get him to stay awake long enough to suck hard enough to be really full. All you do is hold him and nurse him without getting rest or sleep. Try the following survival tips.

Hold a family council with your husband, relatives, and friends who have come to help. Make the following message loud and clear: "We have been blessed with a high-need baby. I need some help. I no longer can cope without your help." You may even read them the Ten Commandments for the Postpartum Mother as listed in Chapter 12. You need someone to hold your baby for you when you manage to get her to nod off to sleep. Your baby needs to be held by someone, but not necessarily always by you. Your husband, a relative, or a friend can relieve you one by one until you get yourself into a system of sleeping when your baby sleeps. High-need babies do cry a lot, but they should not be left to cry *alone*.

Try to learn the knack of nursing in bed so you can doze off when your baby does. You will spend a lot of time in bed in the first few weeks postpartum; so, have a comfortable gown and a robe to wear. One mother of a high-need baby shared with me, "I didn't get dressed in day clothes for three weeks after I came home from the hospital to avoid the temptation to put the baby down and spend that precious time doing housework."

Have a good, nutritious lunch prepared by your husband or a friend waiting in the refrigerator along with snacks to nibble on and liquids to drink throughout the day. Put them on a tray you can eat and drink from while lounging in bed. Take some good books to bed with you that may help you relax or help you get to sleep more easily. Do some needlework, or letter writing, or whatever you enjoy. Your Bible also should be handy for some quiet time with your Lord. The Psalms are a good source of relaxation and meditation for the postpartum mother.

You don't have to stay in bed like an invalid. You can go for a walk outdoors if you find that some physical exercise is relaxing and untiring. Be up and about in your home if you can resist the temptation to get some work done. The reason to stay in bed until the crisis has passed (and it will) is that when you are in bed you are physically resting even if you are not sleeping. You'll be surprised how little catnaps do add up. If you are the type who hates to be in bed "doing nothing," and you are tense and miserable, then get some help learning to relax. Review your childbirth relaxation techniques; have your husband rub your back or give you a massage; and meditate on Scriptures such as Psalm 37:4–5, 7; Proverbs 16:9; Jeremiah 6:16; Philippians 4:6–7; 1 Peter 5:7. Allow yourself the luxury of doing nothing. Pamper yourself. Be good to yourself: put aside all responsibilities except for you and your baby. This is your maternity leave; take it. The housework can be done by someone else, or it can be done next month. Caring for yourself and your baby is your only focus at this time. You actually must put yourself first, maybe for the first time in your life, because your baby depends on you to stay calm, rested, and happy in spirit.

One helpful idea that can give you confidence is to keep a log of the exact times that you and your new baby are sleeping in each twenty-four-hour period. You may be surprised that your baby really is getting enough sleep; remember, what's enough for one baby is only half enough for another baby. You also may be surprised that you are getting as much sleep as you do.

Adapting to the physical demands of breastfeeding and its accompanying schedule is just one of the many changes you will be making in your immediate postpartum period. This period is characterized by numerous physical and emotional changes that can cause undue stress or can be weathered successfully with sufficient information, rest, and support.

Part 4

The
First
Month

CHAPTER 12

POSTPARTUM PARENTING

Bringing home the new baby cements the reality that you are now a family. The euphoria of giving birth begins to wear off, and you as a couple will probably experience some degree of difficulty adjusting to the postpartum period. In the following discussion you will be helped to understand why these feelings occur. With the help of the Lord and the help of her husband, the new mother can cope with these feelings.

Postpartum Changes

"If birth is so wonderful and my baby is a precious gift from God, why do I feel so sad (awful, depressed, upset)?" First of all, mothers, appreciate that you are not alone in your feelings. About 50 percent of all women giving birth in North American hospitals experience some degree of after-baby blues. One hundred thousand women are treated in outpatient clinics for varying degrees of postpartum difficulties and about four thousand women per year are hospitalized with severe psychiatric disturbances within six months after giving birth.

The difference between the "baby blues" and post-partum depression is a matter of timing and degree. Most women experience some degree of temporary baby blues within a week or two after giving birth. These emotional changes are due in part to the fact that often in human adjustment, a low follows a high. From six to eight weeks after birth, actual postpartum depression may occur, manifested by the following signs and symptoms:

- Fatigue
- Episodes of crying, anxiety, and fear
- Confused thoughts and difficulty in concentrating
- Insomnia (even if baby is asleep)
- Periods of nervousness and tension
- Loss of appetite
- Feelings of failure and panic
- Fear of going crazy
- Worry about physical appearance and unattractiveness, with diminishing desire to groom yourself
- Negative feelings toward husband
- Irritation by trivial things—tendency to "make mountains out of mole hills"
- Heart palpitations
- Shaky feelings

In addition, a woman may experience doubt and frustration—doubt about her mothering abilities and frustration at her apparent lack of success. These feelings may lead to despair, which may result in occasional negative feelings toward her baby, which in turn are followed by sensations of guilt for having had these seemingly terrible feelings. Mothers, remember that it is not abnormal (or unchristian) to have these feelings, but it is unhealthy to let them get out of hand. Ventilate these feelings to a trusted person, preferably your husband, and also to your physician.

What Causes Postpartum Depression?

Most postpartum difficulties are caused by too many changes too fast, and depression is the woman's body signal that she has exceeded her physical and psychological capabilities to adapt to these changes. Everyone's capacity to adjust to combined stresses is different. She should not consider this a weakness in herself but realize instead that she has reached a certain stress level exceeding her ability to cope. The usual stresses contributing to postpartum depression are both physical and emotional.

Physical and Chemical Changes

In the postpartum period the woman's body chemistry is going through tremendous fluctuations from the pregnant to the nonpregnant to the lactating states. Her hormones are particularly affected. Changing body chemistry often brings with it changing moods and feelings, and her sleep cycles also have undergone a tremendous change. The mother and father have had to adjust their sleep needs to the cycle of their baby. The sleep-when-your-baby-sleeps advice is indeed necessary for adjusting to the new baby's sleep patterns (or lack of patterns), but this sudden adjustment is not easy for many parents.

Actually, I feel that downright exhaustion either causes or contributes to a slow recovery after giving birth. This is particularly true if, for reasons beyond her control, the mother has experienced a traumatic birth (cesarean section or prolonged and difficult labor in which fear and pain predominated). A difficult physical recovery from birth may be compounded by disappointment that the ideal birth did not occur and expectations were shattered.

Emotional Changes

With the birth of their first children, many women experience status changes. This is particularly true of a very young mother or of a woman who has had an exciting career outside the home from which she received much status and affirmation. A new mother may feel her identity is blurred: "I'm Johnny's mother, and I'm Bob's wife, but what happened to me as a person?" These are normal feelings that any person would have when his or her self-esteem is threatened. Perhaps at no other time in a married couple's life are there as many changes so fast as in the immediate postpartum period: change in lifestyle, role changes for husband and wife, disrupted routines, disrupted sleep patterns, changing economic status, and on and on. Whether most of these changes are for the better or for the worse, the reality is that a lot of the changes bring unusual feelings, which in turn bring the need to cope.

Preventing or Lessening Postpartum Depression

Know Specific Risk Factors

During pregnancy and delivery a woman can identify certain factors that may increase her risk of having postpartum depression.

1. A previous history of depression or difficulty coping with combined stresses
2. Exchanging a high-status career for motherhood, with ambivalent feelings about this status change
3. An unwanted pregnancy and ambivalent feelings of how a child will fit into the current lifestyle
4. Marital discord and unrealistic expectations that a child may solve marital problems
5. A negative birth experience in which fear and pain predominate
6. An ill or premature baby
7. Any situation that separates mother and baby and interferes with a close mother-infant attachment shortly after birth

If you have any of these risk factors, pray and seek counsel during pregnancy and in the early postpartum period.

Make Adequate Preparation

A woman should prepare her heart and body for the coming of her baby by following the suggestions discussed in Chapter 4. During this preparation period she can form relationships with various parenting groups, such as the La Leche League International, that may serve as a positive support group after delivery. Since this type of depression is shared by thousands of other women, women can find comfort from other mothers in these support groups.

Be flexible. When a woman enters the hospital, she should ask God to give her the strength to accept the labor and birth she has even as she plans for the "ideal" delivery. There will always be something about the birth experience that she will want to change "next time."

Ask for rooming-in. Unless a medical complication prevents it, continue the rooming-in started in the hospital (Chapter 7). Mother-infant detachment is one of the contributing factors to postpartum depression. Avoid extreme fatigue at all costs. Although tiredness is a realistic expectation of the parenting profession, new parents can do some things to lessen it, such as obtaining help at home from friends, relatives, or hired help if that is economically feasible. This is a time for Christian friends to rally around the new parents, help with the housework, prepare the meals, and simply "mother" the new mother. In my experience much postpartum fatigue is due less to the many needs of the baby and more to the efforts of the new mother to be all things to all people (see the section "The Father's Postpartum Role" in this chapter).

A new mother must learn how to delegate responsibilities. The housework, cooking, and dishes can be done by someone else, but no one can mother your baby as you can. One new mother with a large family shared with me, "I simply sit in my rocking chair, dressed in my nightgown, nursing my baby and directing traffic." If the baby has older siblings of "working age" (more than four years old), some of the simpler household chores can be delegated to them. Make them feel that they can help Mommy and their new little brother or sister.

The expectant mother should get as much rest as she can in the final months of pregnancy. The final month of pregnancy should be a time of peace and quiet, allowing her to tune in to her unborn child and rest her mind and body for the coming birth. A mother who enters labor tired is likely to be more tired after birth.

Consider yourself. New mothers need to take a few hours out each week to do something for themselves. They may protest, "But my baby needs me all day long." Yes, a new baby does need his or her mother, but she needs herself also. Meeting her own needs is not being selfish or unchristian. It is realizing that only giving is going to wear thin after a while. If she feels good about herself as a person, she will be more effective as a mother, and her child ultimately will profit.

The special time a mother saves for herself should be spent on a relaxing activity, some physical exercise, a hobby, or just a peaceful walk in the park. This special time is analogous to a doctor's going off call. A doctor who never signs out to a trusted colleague and goes off call will soon experience burnout and become less effective as a doctor. In reality, a nursing mother can never go off call completely; but she can sign out occasionally to a trusted mother-substitute during brief periods when her baby has fewer needs. (I admit this is more easily said than done.) Fathers make the best mother-substitutes and they are handy—they come home from work every day. That's the time to take a soak in a bubble bath (together if baby is asleep!). At the very least, mothers, don't often "waste" the baby's naptimes on housework. A good book (for those who love reading) can be read in snatches, even while breastfeeding (if you can tear your eyes away from your baby's face). This is also a good time to pray.

Keep yourself attractive. If a woman looks good, she most likely will feel good. Give proper attention to good grooming even if you have to force yourself to take a weekly trip to the beauty parlor, if that is what you did before baby. Or get a manicure or a new haircut or buy a new lipstick. Join forces with a close friend who can be trusted to see ways you can stay beautiful.

Have a balanced diet. Your doctor may advise you to continue your prenatal vitamins. Avoid junk food because it may cause blood-sugar swings and contribute to postpartum blues. If you are nursing, you will need the same nutritious calories and balanced diet that you needed during pregnancy. Postpartum weight loss should occur mainly by increased exercise and not by crash diets. Dietary deficiencies may contribute to postpartum depression, especially combined with the stresses of pregnancy, giving birth, and new-parent fatigue. A consultation with a nutritionist who is experienced in postpartum problems may be necessary. Ask your doctor or midwife for a referral. A nutritional consultant can be helpful for any new mother. Ask at your hospital about having an appointment before you leave the hospital, or arrange for it when the baby is several weeks old and you feel like getting out.

Avoid too many visitors. In the first few weeks after coming home, limit visitors. "Thou shalt not entertain" is one of the commandments for a new mother. Remember, "Help" (even if it's your mother) is to *help you* and is not to be entertained. The helping person should know you are going to care for the baby most of the time; she is there to care for the household duties and other routine matters. Clarify this ahead of time to avoid hurt feelings. Make a written list if it is hard for you to tell this person what things need to be done. Being all things to all people is what gets a new mother overly tired.

Avoid isolation. Seek out friends and visitors when you want them. Surround yourself with positive people. Avoid negative advisers who may try to pressure you into a mothering style that does not feel right to you. Mothering in a way that basically goes against your God-given intuition (the unique blueprint for mothering your own child) is a setup for postpartum depression. The human, emotional organism is not equipped to operate constantly outside God's basic design. Any advice that does not feel right to you and is not working should be dropped.

Exercise. Force yourself to get at least a half hour of sustained exercise each day even if it is simply walking in the park with your baby in a front carrier. Physical exercise is absolutely mandatory for a new mother. Tiny babies are very portable. Nothing in the mother-infant contract says you must stay home all the time. Home to a tiny baby is where his or her parents are.

Involve your husband. Be specific in telling your husband what you need (laundry or dishes done, a housekeeper, help with the other children, and so on). Remember, your husband is undergoing some postpartum adjustment difficulties of his own. Quite honestly, many men are slow to sense exactly what new mothers need, so you simply may have to make your needs known in a nice way but also loud and clear! Your husband may perceive a situation as tiny and insignificant and therefore ignore it, but to you it is a major need. Tell him.

Avoid drugs. In my experience, drugs are not the answer to postpartum depression. Unless your depression requires hospitalization, try to avoid drugs altogether.

The Father's Postpartum Role

Fathers, your wife needs mothering too. Be tuned in and sensitive to her physical and emotional needs. If your wife is having a problem with a status change, help her feel she has stepped up the ladder of personal worth and not down. Constantly express genuine love and support, "You are doing the most important job in the world, mothering our child."

Beware of the many physical and emotional changes going on within your wife. This is a time of sincere, high-level communication in which you sympathize with her feelings: "You must feel very tired. I understand. How can I help?" Also realize that your wife may be somewhat reluctant to ask for your help since she may feel this is a sign of maternal weakness. She may be trying to act like supermother: the perfect wife, the perfect mother, the perfect hostess, the perfect housekeeper, the perfect everything.

Everything drains on the new mother. The responsibility falls to the father to be sure the mother is not totally drained. Even in the economically poor cultures in the world a new mother is given a *doula* (from the Greek word meaning "servant"). A *doula* is a person who can take over the household chores and free the new mother to be a mother. Anyone can be a *doula* to the new mother, even the father. If your friends ask, "Is there anything you need?" answer, "Yes, please bring over supper tonight."

Be sensitive to signs. Be sensitive to the early signs of depression: insomnia, loss of appetite, unfounded nagging, lessening attention to grooming, not wanting to get out of the house. If these red flags appear, take steps immediately. Seek prayer and professional counsel before these early warning signs progress into a full-blown depression and you wind up being both mother and father while your wife is recovering in the hospital.

Respect the nesting instinct. During the final month of pregnancy and for the first few months after birth, the mother needs a stable nest. Avoid making major changes near the time of childbirth. This is not the time to change jobs or move into a new house or move across the country. Remember, the nesting instinct is very strong in a new mother.

Control visitors. Be sure that well-meaning friends and relatives help instead of hinder the new mother. An overextended visit in the first few weeks can be very draining, especially when baby has been up a lot at night. The new mother needs time to rest or sleep rather than entertain yet another visitor. If someone comes at a bad time, say so.

Care for older children. Take charge of most of the physical maintenance of the older children. This frees your wife to concentrate on their emotional needs, which often go up when a new baby arrives; they also want mother's prime time.

Show love. Convey your love for your wife. You may say, "Of course I love my wife." But do you show it? Because of the previously mentioned reasons, your wife will have problems with her self-esteem during the postpartum adjustment period. One of the greatest gifts you can give your child is to show love to his or her mother.

Seek prayer and counsel. The principles of Christian natural childbirth should lower the risks of postpartum depression since you have begun relying on the Lord for strength even during your pregnancy. The following Scripture passages are selected readings for depressed mothers who rely on the Lord for their strength:

Psalm 46:1	Psalm 34:18
Psalm 42:5	Nehemiah 8:10
Jeremiah 29:11	Isaiah 26:3
Psalm 9:9–10	John 14:27
Psalm 107:28–29	Psalm 27:5
1 Peter 5:7	2 Timothy 1:7
Ephesians 4:23–24	Psalm 34:4
1 Chronicles 28:20	Isaiah 41:10

Ten Commandments for the Postpartum Mother

1. Thou shalt not give up thy baby to strange caregivers.
2. Thou shalt not cook, clean house, do laundry, or entertain.
3. Thou shalt be given a *doula*.
4. Thou shalt remain clothed in thy nightgown and sit in thy rocking chair.
5. Thou shalt honor thy husband with his share of household chores.
6. Thou shalt take long walks in green pastures, eat good food, and drink much water.
7. Thou shalt not have before you strange and unhelpful visitors.
8. Thou shalt groom thy hair and adorn thy body with attractive robes.

9. Thou shalt be allowed to sleep when baby sleeps.
10. Look to the Lord, and He will give you strength: thou shalt not have prophets of bad baby advice before you.

Bibliography

The following books and reference sources are arranged according to their major subjects, although many of them cover a wide range of topics on parenting. Please bear in mind that when recommending a book, *I am not necessarily endorsing every statement made in it.* I have chosen to recommend those books that, in my opinion, contain important messages that will contribute to your growth as Christian parents. Not all of the books on the following list are specifically Christian, but they are not non-Christian either. I have also chosen those books most in accordance with the philosophy of attachment and feeling right that I have continually advocated in this book.

Abortion

Schaeffer, Francis A. and C. Everett Koop. *Whatever Happened to the Human Race?* Westchester, IL: Crossway, 1983.

> Written by the late renowned Christian philosopher and the former surgeon general of the United States, this book is a real must for understanding the issues surrounding abortion, and it exposes the rapid but subtle loss of human rights.

Swindoll, Charles. *Sanctity of Life: The Inescapable Issue.* Dallas, TX: Word, 1990.

Besides the sanctity of life, Swindoll examines abortion after the fact and makes a plea for morality and the resolve to be strong.

Wilke, Dr. J. C. and Mrs. *Abortion: Questions and Answers.* Cincinnati, OH: Hayes Publishing, 1989.
If you could choose only one book this should be it: a reference manual with questions and answers on all the aspects of abortion.

Breastfeeding

Breastfeeding Organizations. La Leche League International, Inc., 1-800-LA LECHE, P.O. Box 4079, Schaumberg, IL 60168.
This organization not only teaches better mothering through breastfeeding but teaches better mothering in all aspects of parenting and child care. There is a local La Leche League in every major city in the United States and throughout the world. Write for a free catalog of their breastfeeding publications, which contains nearly one hundred books and booklets on all aspects of parenting.

Breastfeeding Your Baby: A Mother's Guide.
A one-hour video produced by Medela, Inc., (the breast pump company) in cooperation with La Leche League. William Sears, M.D., Jay Gordon, M.D., celebrities, and breastfeeding experts instruct and encourage; families speak on breastfeeding's benefits. Available through La Leche League.

Bumgarner, Norma Jane. *Mothering Your Nursing Toddler.* Schaumberg, IL: La Leche League International, Inc., 1982.
Not only does this book extol the virtues of nursing the toddler and not weaning the child before his time, it is a beautiful account of attachment mothering.

Kippley, Sheila. *Breastfeeding and Natural Child Spacing*. The Couple to Couple League International, Inc., P.O. Box 111184, Cincinnati, OH 45211.
  This book discusses the concept of natural mothering and how it can postpone the return of fertility.

Torgus, Judy, ed. *The Womanly Art of Breastfeeding*. Schaumberg, IL: La Leche League International, Inc., 1987.
  The authority for the breastfeeding mother, this book not only deals with the joys and problems of breastfeeding but also affirms the profession of attachment mothering.

Childbirth

Brewer, Gail Sforza and Tom Brewer, M.D. *What Every Pregnant Woman Should Know: The Truth About Diet and Drugs in Pregnancy*. New York: Viking-Penguin, 1985.
  The importance of good nutrition in pregnancy. Relationship of toxemia and diet in pregnancy.

Dick-Read, Grantly. *Childbirth Without Fear.* (5th ed.) Edited by Helen Wessel. New York: Harper and Row, 1984.
  This is a classic book on natural childbirth that demonstrates how laboring women can overcome the fear-tension-pain cycle.

Evans, Debra. *The Complete Book on Childbirth*. Wheaton, IL: Tyndale House, 1986.
  This book is valuable for the original and beautifully expressed concepts on marriage and birth. Her information on breastfeeding is insufficient and I do not completely agree with her attitudes toward pain and childbirth. Readers will want to balance this book with others on Christian childbirth and breastfeeding.

Korte, Diana and Roberta Scaer. *A Good Birth, A Safe Birth*. New York: Bantam, 1990.

This basic guide to childbirth options helps expectant parents negotiate to get the kind of birth experience they want. Also provides insight into recent trends in childbirth.

MacNutt, Francis and Judith. *Praying for Your Unborn Child: How Parents' Prayers Can Make a Difference in the Health and Happiness of Their Children.* New York: Doubleday, 1989.

A beautiful and insightful guide to praying for your baby during each stage of pregnancy, from conception to delivery. The authors show how parents who surround their unborn infant with love, prayer, and serenity will profoundly affect their child's personality and well-being.

McCutcheon-Rosegg, Susan and Peter Rosegg. *Natural Childbirth the Bradley Way.* New York: E. P. Dutton-Penguin, 1984.

An updated guide to pregnancy and childbirth. Step-by-step preparations are provided for the couple looking for a totally natural, drug-free birth.

Nilsson, Lennart. *A Child Is Born.* (Rev. ed.) New York: Delacourt, 1990. Also published by Life Education, reprint no. 27. Canaan, NH: Media International.

A series of unprecedented photographs of the development of the embryo, from conception to birth, the book will help you realize the true miracle of fetal development and how a Supreme Architect is certainly in charge of this development.

Noble, Elizabeth. *Having Twins: A Parent's Guide to Pregnancy, Birth and Early Childhood.* Boston, MA: Houghton-Mifflin, 1991.

A veteran childbirth expert tells how to carry healthy babies to term.

Odent, Michael, M.D. *Birth Reborn.* New York: Random House, 1984.

A beautifully illustrated description of birth at Pithiviers in France, using explicit photography to help demonstrate how birth is best achieved in the modified (standing) squat position and also with the aid of tubs. The description of how birth can be a normal, safe, and confident part of life encourages couples in planning the birth they want.

Sears, William M. and Linda H. Holt. *The Pregnancy Book: A Month-by-Month Guide*. New York: Little Brown Co., 1997.

Wessel, Helen. *Natural Childbirth and the Christian Family*. Bookmates International, Inc., Apple Tree Family Ministries, P.O. Box 2083, Artesia, CA 90702–2083, 562-925-0149.

A must for all parents who are taking prepared-childbirth classes. Mrs. Wessel, a mother of six, adds a Christian perspective to the childbirth-without-fear techniques described by Dr. Grantly Dick-Read.

_____. *Under the Apple Tree*. Fresno, CA: Bookmates International, Inc., 1982. (See above for address to write for booklet.)

An absolute must for Christian parents-to-be. Mrs. Wessel discusses the scriptural basis of marriage, birthing, and early parenting practices; it should be read and studied by husband and wife together.

Discipline

Craig, Sydney. *Raising Your Child Not by Force but by Love*. Philadelphia, PA: The Westminster Press, 1973.

This book, written from a Christian perspective, helps parents gain an understanding of discipline as a *positive* concept. It has great insight into the feelings of children and the effect of our discipline (good and bad) on their feelings. It also gives insight into why we get angry with our children and alternative ways of expressing and managing anger.

Crary, Elizabeth. *Without Spanking or Spoiling*. Seattle, WA: Parenting Press, 1979.
Alternatives for parents to recognize and attain their personal goals in childrearing.

_____. *Kids Can Cooperate: A Practical Guide to Teaching Problem Solving*. Seattle, WA: Parenting Press, 1984.
Teaches children skills to solve conflicts themselves.

_____. *Pick Up Your Socks . . . And Other Skills Growing Children Need*. Seattle, WA: Parenting Press, 1990.
Teaches children responsibility skills.

Faber, Adele and Elaine Mazlish. *Siblings Without Rivalry*. New York: Avon, 1987.
Help your children live together so you can live too.

_____. *How to Talk So Kids Will Listen and Listen So Kids Will Talk*. New York: Avon, 1982.
Communication skills for parents: how to listen and deal with feelings; alternatives to nagging and punishment.

Fennema, Jack. *Nurturing Children in the Lord*. Phillipsburg, NJ: Presbyterian and Reformed Publishing, 1977.
A study guide on developing a biblical approach to discipline, this is an excellent book for Christian parents who wish to base their discipline on scriptural principles.

Kesler, Jay. *Too Big to Spank*. Ventura, CA: Regal, 1978.
This is a practical guide for parents to help them discipline and build self-esteem in their teenager.

Leman, Kevin. *Making Children Mind Without Losing Yours*. Old Tappan, NJ: Revell, 1984.
Should have been titled *Helping Children Mind* by Dr. Leman's own admission. A practical, commonsense approach to discipline based on action (but rarely spanking), not words. Called Reality Discipline, it teaches children to be accountable for their actions.

Only one area of concern: Dr. Leman advises parents to leave their young babies at home so they can get out now and then. I encourage couples to get out together and take baby too.

Narramore, S. Bruce. *Help! I'm a Parent*. Grand Rapids, MI: Zondervan, 1972.

This book applies both psychological and biblical principles in arriving at a systematic approach to discipline.

Sears, William M. and Martha Sears. *The Discipline Book: Everything You Need to Know to Have a Better Behaved Child*. New York: Little Brown Co., 1995.

Stewart, Blaize Clement. *The Loving Parent: A Guide to Growing Up Before Your Children Do*. San Luis Obispo, CA: Impact, 1988.

A secular book dealing sensitively with issues such as obedience, lying, stealing, cheating, anger, and sexuality.

Divorce

Hart, Archibald D. *Children and Divorce—What to Expect, How to Help*. Waco, TX: Word, 1982.

Written by a Christian psychologist, this realistic and helpful guidebook helps divorcing parents understand their children's feelings and help them cope.

Smith, Virginia Watts. *The Single Parent*. Old Tappan, NJ: Revell, 1979.

This very sensitive Christian guide to the plight of the single parent offers sympathetic understanding and practical advice on the dilemma of achieving personal fulfillment and rearing a child for Christ.

Education

Elkind, David. *The Hurried Child, Growing Up Too Fast, Too Soon*. Reading, MA: Addison-Wesley, 1989.

Offers insight and advice on the burden of stress on modern children who are "forced to bloom."

Harris, Gregg. *The Christian Home School.* Brentwood, TN: Wolgemuth & Hyatt, 1987.
A good starter book for families considering home school.

Macauley, Susan Schaeffer. *For the Children's Sake: Foundations of Education for Home and School.* Westchester, IL: Crossway, 1987.
The daughter of the late Christian philosopher Francis A. Schaeffer, who grew up in Switzerland and L'Abri Fellowship, writes about the wonderful, life-enriching, joyous experience education can be for your child, in your home and in school.

Montessori, Maria. *The Discovery of the Child.* New York: Ballantine, 1967.
A good explanation of the Montessori philosophy of education, this book defines the needs and offers practical education suggestions for the various sensitive periods of the child.

Moore, Raymond S. and Dorothy N. *Home Grown Kids.* Waco, TX: Word, 1981.
A practical handbook for teaching your children at home, this book calls attention to the fact that education is still the prime responsibility of the parent. The educational suggestions are provocative and well worth considering; however, I do not agree with some of the authors' suggestions on early child care, especially much of their nutritional advice.

Sears, William M. and L. Thompson. *The A.D.D. Book: Attention Deficit Disorder.* New York: Little Brown Co., 1998.

Uphoff, James K., June E. Gilmore, and Rosemarie Huber. *Summer Children—Ready or Not for School.* J & J

Publishing Co., P.O. Box 8549, Middletown, OH 45042.

Marriage

Crabb, Lawrence Jr. *How to Become One with Your Mate*. Grand Rapids, MI: Zondervan, 1982.
> This is a small, very readable excerpt from *The Marriage Builder,* by Lawrence Crabb, on oneness of body and spirit in the marriage relationship. Looking to Christ to fulfill our needs enables us to minister to our mates.

Harley, Willard. *His Needs, Her Needs: Building an Affair-Proof Marriage*. Old Tappan, NJ: Revell, 1986.
> Identifies the ten most important marital needs of husbands and wives and teaches how those needs can be fulfilled.

Wheat, Ed, M.D. and Gloria Okes Perkins. *Love Life for Every Married Couple*. Grand Rapids, MI: Zondervan, 1980.
> How to fall in love, stay in love, rekindle your love.

Media

Farah, Joseph (editor). *Between the Lines*. 325 Pennsylvania Ave., SE, Washington, DC 20003.
> A biweekly newsletter covering the politics and morality of the news media and entertainment industry.

Lappe, Francis Moore. *What to Do After You Turn Off the TV*. New York: Ballantine, 1985.

For other information concerning media write:

> Christian Leaders for Responsible Television
> c/o American Family Association
> P.O. Box 2440
> Tupelo, MS 38803

Mother-Infant Attachment

Fraiberg, Selma. "Every Child's Birthright." In *Selected Writings of Selma Fraiberg*. Louis Fraiberg, editor. Columbus, OH: Ohio State University Press, 1987.

Kaplan, Louise. *Oneness and Separateness: From Infant to Individual*. New York: Simon and Schuster, 1978.
> A beautiful discussion of the inner workings of the child as he goes from oneness to separateness. Dr. Kaplan explores some of the theory of the benefits of mother-infant attachment and the consequences of premature detachment.

Klaus and Kennell. *Parent-Infant Bonding*. Saint Louis, MO: C. V. Mosby, 1982.
> This book discusses results of studies that suggest the positive benefits of mother and baby remaining in close contact with each other immediately after birth.

McClure, Vimala Schneider. *Infant Massage*. New York: Bantam, 1989.
> Teaches parents to discover the joys and benefits of massage for their babies and for themselves. Photographs illustrate each step of the process. Massage promotes bonding, reduces tension and fussing, and aids in physical development. I highly recommend this book.

Montagu, Ashley. *Touching: The Human Significance of the Skin*. New York: Harper and Row, 1986.
> The classical treatise on the importance of the skin as the largest organ of human sensation. Dr. Montagu discusses at length the psychological benefits of skin-to-skin contact.

Natural Family Planning

Kass-Annese, Barbara, R.N., N.P., and Hal Danzer, M.D. *The Fertility Awareness Workbook*. New York: Putnam, 1981.

A concise, how-to book on natural family planning. Good illustrations and diagrams.

Kippley, Sheila. *Breastfeeding and Natural Child Spacing*. Cincinnati, OH: The Couple to Couple League International, Inc., 1989.

This book discusses the concept of natural mothering and how it can postpone the return of fertility.

Kippley, John and Sheila. *The Art of Natural Family Planning*. Cincinnati, OH: The Couple to Couple League International, Inc., 1989.

To be used either on your own or as part of an instructional program, the book teaches the sympto-thermal method of fertility control. Part One explains the "why" of NFP; Part Two the "how to." My favorite chapter is entitled "Marriage Building with NFP."

New Age

Kjos, Barit. *Your Child and the New Age*. Wheaton, IL: Victor, 1990.

A solid explanation of various aspects of the New Age influence in schools and media, with practical suggestions on what parents can do. Issues such as counterfeit spirituality, values clarification, New Age globalism in schools, mind manipulation, distortion of imagination, pagan sentiments in toys, TV, movies, reading material, and music.

Michaelsen, Johanna. *Like Lambs to the Slaughter: Your Child and the Occult*. Eugene, OR: Harvest House, 1989.

Information parents need to have to help their children survive or avoid the subtle and not-so-subtle New Age influences in the world today.

Parenting and Child Care

Cahill, Mary Ann. *The Heart Has Its Own Reasons*. New York: New American Library, 1985.

This book encourages mothers to stay home with their children and gives practical and timely suggestions on how that can be managed financially.

Campbell, D. Ross. *How to Really Love Your Child*. Wheaton, IL: Victor, 1978.
This book, written by a Christian psychiatrist, discusses the importance of touching, eye-to-eye contact, and focused attention. It offers practical tips on how to convey your love to your child.

————. *How to Really Love Your Teenager*. Wheaton, IL: Victor, 1981.
Encouraging guidance for parents struggling to understand and express love to their teens. Picks up where *How to Really Love Your Child* leaves off.

Crook, William G. and Laura J. Stevens. *Solving the Puzzle of Your Hard to Raise Child*. New York: Random House, 1987.
Parents of high-need children need the information in this book concerning the effect on behavior of improper or inadequate nutrition. Tells how to improve the child's diet and, therefore, his behavior.

Dobson, James. *Hide or Seek*. Tappan, NJ: Revell, 1979.
In my opinion this is the best of Dr. Dobson's many books. It deals with the extremely important issue of how to build self-esteem in your child.

————. *Preparing for Adolescence*. New York: Bantam, 1980.
An excellent text for parent and preteen to share, with an accompanying study guide for your child. I've used it as each of our first four approached their teen years.

Noble, Elizabeth. *Having Twins: A Parent's Guide to Pregnancy, Birth, and Early Childhood*. Boston, MA: Houghton-Mifflin, 1991.

A veteran childbirth expert tells how to carry healthy babies to term.

Sears, William M. and Martha Sears. *The Baby Book: Everything You Need to Know About Your Baby—From Birth to Age Two*. New York: Little Brown Co., 1993.

_____. *Becoming a Father: How to Nurture and Enjoy Your Family*. Schaumberg, IL: La Leche League International, 1986.

_____. *Growing Together: A Parents' Guide to Baby's First Year*. Schaumberg, IL: La Leche League International, 1987.
This book describes the month-by-month development of babies from birth to one year.

_____. *Nighttime Parenting*. Schaumberg, IL: La Leche League International, 1987.
Practical tips for parenting your child to sleep.

_____. *Parenting the Fussy Baby and High Need Child*. New York: Little Brown Co., 1996.

_____. *SIDS: A Parent's Guide to Understanding and Preventing the Sudden Infant Death Syndrome*. New York: Little Brown Co., 1995.

Sex Education

Andry, Andrew and Stephen Schepp. *How Babies Are Made*. New York: Little-Brown, 1984.
This is the perfect starter book for teaching the reproductive process to your children. Illustrated with paper sculpture, figures are realistic and simple. Begins with plants and animals, and tastefully illustrates humans, for ages 3–10. Ends with the mother breastfeeding her baby.

Kitzinger, Sheila and Lennart Nilsson. *Being Born*. New York: Grosset Dunlap, 1986.

BIBLIOGRAPHY

The same magnificent photos of Nilssons's *A Child Is Born* combined with poetic text about conception and birth make this book timeless. Adults as well as children are drawn to it, even though it is written for children.

McDowell, Josh and Dick Day. *Why Wait? What You Need to Know About the Teen Sexuality Crisis.* San Bernardino, CA: Here's Life Publishers, 1987.
A very frank look at the situation challenging teens and the biblical perspective on what God wants for their lives in regard to chastity.

Sexuality

Evans, Debra. *The Mystery of Womanhood.* Westchester, IL: Crossway, 1987.
A biblical perspective on being a woman, finding the inner beauty of femininity, handling stress of daily living, fertility and childbearing, sexuality in a healthy marriage, and living with a cyclical nature.

Penner, Clifford and Joyce. *The Gift of Sex: A Christian Guide to Sexual Fulfillment.* Waco, TX: Word, 1981.
A comprehensive and joyful guide to sex for Christians.

Sleep Problems

Sears, William. *Nighttime Parenting.* Schaumberg, IL: La Leche League International, 1987.
Practical tips for parenting your child to sleep.

Thevenin, Tine. *The Family Bed.* New York: Avery, 1987.
This book brings back an age-old concept in child rearing and advocates children sleeping with their parents or with other siblings as a way to solve bedtime problems, create a closer bond within the family, and give children a greater sense of security.

Your Child's Devotional Life

Blitchington, Evelyn. *The Family Devotions Idea Book*. Minneapolis, MN: Bethany House, 1982.
This book is full of practical ideas on how to conduct meaningful family devotions.

Chapin, Alice. *Building Your Child's Faith*. Nashville, TN: Thomas Nelson, 1990.
Simple, fun ideas for teaching children how to pray, worship, and discover the Bible.

Haystead, Wes. *Teaching Your Child About God*. Ventura, CA: Regal, 1981.
This is an easy-to-read book with practical advice on the spiritual training of the child at various stages.

BIBLIOGRAPHY

Your Child's Emotional Life

Blankenhorn, David. *Fatherless America.* New York: Basic
Books, 1995.
This book is full of historical background to explain the
absence of many fathers today.

Maurer, Adah. *Sparing the Child.* New York: Basic Books,
1994.
*Simple nutrition ideas for the busy children how to eat
nutritious, and discover the magic.*

Lew and Wold, Barbara. *The Good Manners book.* Guiford,
CT: Rizzoli, 1981.
This is an easy-to-read book, with parent advice and
the applications of the child at school.

About the Authors

William Sears, M.D., and his wife, Martha Sears, R.N., have more than two decades of professional pediatric experience. Dr. Sears is clinical assistant professor of pediatrics at the University of Southern California School of Medicine and a practicing pediatrician. Martha Sears is a registered nurse and a certified childbirth educator.

They have cared for more than ten thousand babies, including eight of their own. Dr. Sears has written twelve books on raising children, including five with his wife.

LOOK FOR THESE OTHER BOOKS IN THE SEARS PARENTING LIBRARY